How to Live Abroad and Thrive with Passive Income

PIERRE BLAKE

DEDICATION

To all of those that genuinely listened to and supported
me, it truly means everything, thank you.

CONTENTS

CHAPTER 1
MY STORY

In all of the six foreign countries that I've lived in, all have proven to be extremely transformative self-development experiences. These times living abroad allowed, and sometimes forced, me to grow more than I ever would've thought initially possible. Countless adventures which were full of true excitement and enjoyment and all of them constantly pushed me out of my comfort zone, into uncharted territories. With each obstacle I was able to overcome, there came rewarding lessons about life.

I'll be the first to admit that when I started, I had no idea what I was doing and learned as I went. There were times where I definitely smashed my head into more than a few walls, metaphorically speaking of course. Over the years, after building up all of the experience of living in several countries, I was able to create and perfect strategies which allowed me not only to survive but thrive.

How to Live Abroad and Thrive with Passive Income is the ultimate guide book designed so you can get the absolute most out of your move abroad. The strategies that I have perfected eliminate stresses that would typically come from packing up all your personal possessions, moving to the other side of the planet, and starting a new life. The focus is on crafting a sustainable and immensely rewarding life abroad. Without having the proper strategies in place, you might be stuck as a permanent outsider in your new home, never able to make the most of your situation, or be forced to return to your home country because the financial burden has become too large to handle.

I'm not just going to teach you how to move to a foreign country and barely scrape by as a poor English teacher, that's not my style. Instead, I'll share my strategies that teach how to give your life complete freedom, mainly through entrepreneurship and passive income, but also through efficient lifestyle design, so all your ducks are in a row.

Some of the obstacles that I will cover in this book include choosing your destination, creating a detailed budget, powerful ways to save the most money as possible, reducing personal possessions with minimalism, generating both passive and active incomes, and life strategies that will teach you how to meet people and not miss any valuable opportunities that may arise along the way.

Hopefully, I've got your attention. Through what I've learned over the years, my lifestyle has afforded me complete freedom of my time, so I can focus on what I want, work when I want, all while living where I want for the last 8.5 years. Nowadays, I wake up every day excited to pursue my greatest dreams, focusing on projects that I want to focus on, and not someone else's. If I want to live in a tropical climate and take an afternoon nap every day, then that's what I'm going to do! My greatest "problems" in life have become choosing where I'd like to live next or where I will eat lunch.

Living in foreign countries can be incredibly exciting and rewarding when done right. If you don't know how to do it, it's easy to make decisions that will take away from, instead of add to the experience. Looking at the whole move from a distance can be incredibly scary, and that's the main reason why most people don't even attempt moving in the first place. As I have more and more discussions with people around the world, who are interested in my lifestyle, I always tend to get asked the same questions, again and again. The main concerns tend to be about how to make money sustainably while living abroad, how to meet people when you don't know anyone, and how to successfully participate in a foreign society without knowing the language. Don't you worry your little head, through trial and error, the head banging I was talking about, I've developed a plethora of proven strategies that I will cover in depth in the coming chapters that make all of these concerns melt away, like butter on a hot skillet.

A little back story about me, my name is Pierre Blake, and ten years ago, my life was not so perfect, imagine that. I was shy and not getting the most out of my university experience, where I felt incredibly stuck in a highly-monotonous and unfulfilling dorm life. Every day I would go to class, eat in the dorm cafeterias, which were actually tasty, and then retreat to the safe haven of my dorm room, where I would focus alone on my hobbies. I'd spend a lot of my time desperately wanting to meet new people but found myself generally too shy to do so. Sounds exciting right? I sure knew how to live it up!

On one of the many monotonous days, while going through my daily campus life, I stumbled upon promotional material for the university's study abroad programs. At that point, my university had been really pumping out their exchange program propaganda. They claimed to have one of the largest study abroad programs in the whole of the United States; I thought I'd put them to the test.

Ever since I was a wee lad, I often fantasized about living as an international man of mystery, a life on the road, full of adventure! I didn't know it at the time, but I was able to make that childhood dream a reality. Back then, I knew I wanted to explore the world, but I didn't think it was going to be possible until much later in life.

From the day I stepped foot into the study abroad office, my entire life took on a whole new trajectory. There were so many different countries to choose from I didn't know where to start. Eventually, I used my tried-and-true method I discovered when I was a boy and choosing which Pokémon card packages to buy at the store. The technique went a little bit something like this: when I was young, we are talking 10 or 11 here folks, I wasn't an adult Pokémon collector, I would lay out the sealed Pokémon card packages in front of me. You can imagine an incredibly cute young man taking his little man hand and raising it to hover above each card package without touching them. I'd close my little eyes and feel the energy of each package of cards, eventually stopping on the one that felt the best, and buy that package.

When it came to the process of choosing study exchange programs, it was like I went back to my childhood and was choosing Pokémon cards. There was a paper with a long list of exchange programs listed on it, I closed my eyes and ran my finger down the list of exchange programs until the energy felt right. When I stopped and slowly opened my eyes with much anticipation, I saw that my now 19-year-old finger was resting on Bangkok, Thailand!

I knew absolutely jack squat about Thailand! I knew it was in Asia, that large landmass on the opposite side of the planet, but that was about it. A few months later and I was on my first long-haul overseas flight, which turned into a dramatic adventure of its own, enjoying unlimited alcohol, getting wasted. Long story short, at my Air India connection in New Delhi, the airline lost the entire flight's tickets and ended up handwriting each one after I personally and frantically prodded them in a scene of complete chaos. I was off to a smooth start!

The semester I spent abroad ended up being the most transformative period of my entire existence as a human being. Constantly, I was forced to step out of my comfort zone, into the unknown, where I realized extreme personal development while I broke down all of the barriers that I had built up over my 20 years as a wee boy. I was forced to change in so many ways, and even though at times it was incredibly challenging, I mean seriously hard, I never regret anything because I know it all made me a much better person in the end.

Experiences that pushed me the hardest were by being constantly forced into difficult social situations. Whether it was in order to function in my new daily life abroad, make new friends from around the world with strangers, or finally get over my fear of rejection by approaching beautiful women, it all sculpted me into the man here today like a sculpture of a Greek god. I am forever thankful to my study abroad friends who pushed me to try, giving me a much-needed confidence boost for the rest of my life.

I was finally forced, thankfully, to turn into an extrovert instead of the introvert I had been for the previous 20 years of my life. This transformation did not occur without a fight, there were some extremely tough times to overcome, but it's almost like I had no choice, fight or flight. When it's time for something to happen in life, it tends just to happen. I couldn't help but be forced out of my comfort zone and forced to grow in my new foreign environment. Somehow, deep down, I knew that I always wanted to be the person I was morphing into like a Power Ranger. My evil master plan was working!

My life changed for the better when I decided to go after what I truly wanted when I wanted it. At that point, I never created any more regrets. After pushing through and conquering all of these new challenges, exploring several countries during my exchange program, and meeting the people from all of the various countries, I learned that the world wasn't such a scary place after all, like the news media wanted me to think. I learned that even though people may look different, we all pretty much want the same things in life, such as love and purpose. I developed a sense of self-worth, compassion, and confidence that nobody can ever take from me.

Ten years on and I now have the life that I always dreamed of. Since I began that first trip to Bangkok, I've opened myself up to new experiences that would've never been possible to take advantage of if I wasn't living the lifestyle I had created. I'm constantly being thrown into situations where I meet interesting people and their cultures while learning a lot in the process.

I had many unique experiences like joining a group of wealthy Korean businessmen for a night out of eating super expensive raw fish, singing horribly in private karaoke bars, and being driven from place to place in a Maybach with a private driver. I doubt that would have happened if I stayed in rural Michigan.

I'm free from having a boss telling me what to do or where to go and can do anything I want all on my own timeline. For the ten years following the exchange program, I have lived in several foreign countries including Thailand, Japan, Hong Kong, South Korea, China, and Vietnam. In 2014, I began my food, travel, and lifestyle blog, and a few years later I became a full-time blogger and now author. No time restrictions mean I can stay in any country as long as I want unless they throw me out.

When I'm blogging, I'm generally not paying for accommodation, so my lifestyle of living high on the hog at luxury hotels is way cheaper than if I was paying rent, even when you factor in airfare. For example, last year I stayed in the United Arab Emirates for a month and spent less than $100 USD for the duration of the stay, while I lived like a millionaire, more on this in later chapters.

Even before becoming a full-time travel blogger, I still was living abroad with a lifestyle of freedom which was completely location independent, meaning I could make money regardless of my location. The focus was always on being creative with my work so I could pursue my own businesses such as web design, photography, videography, online marketing, audio production, book publishing, acting, stock trading, real estate investment, and so much more.

Don't worry if you don't have tons of creative skills, it doesn't mean your chances are ruined from having a lifestyle of freedom abroad. Anyone can use the strategies outlined in this book to create a lifestyle that works for them. What I'll focus on in the coming chapters is how to maximize your individual skill-set with your interests in mind, so you can turn your strengths into your own business. You'll be able to enjoy your work and be able to live with purpose.

I could've gone on with my own businesses indefinitely, but there was a point where I just couldn't stand working with clients any longer. If you didn't know, being a professional creative, such as a photographer, videographer or designer, and having clients that think they know your craft better than you is a very stressful endeavor. I'd often wonder why someone is hiring me if they think that they can do my job better than me? Instead of continuing these businesses with all of the pesky clients, I decided to utilize all of my skills on my own project, which was the PIERREBLAKE.com blog. No more people telling me how to do my job! Now, all of my previous business skills and hobbies could be put to use in one master plan that I created.

During all of my time living and thriving abroad, I've never run out of money. With my strategies, there was never a time where I was forced to change my plans because of income. Everything I've developed is completely sustainable allowing for ways to consistently build savings as well as maintain a life full of adventure and freedom.

Currently, at age 30, I have a handful of passive income streams that make me enough money to afford my living expenses in practically any developed country I would like to live in, which also allows me to save money in the process.

What this actually looks like in my day to day life is that I can spend just a few hours here and there managing my passive income streams; then I'm able to take the majority of my time and focus on projects that I'm more passionate about, like this book, because I care about you and love you eternally. This was a lifestyle that I built from scratch all by myself. After tweaking it over the years, I've been able to realize many benefits that it has brought to my life. I am confident that you will be able to replicate my results without too many hang-ups if you just stick to the script. The great thing about it is that you don't need to have any certain occupation, such as being a travel blogger, to achieve anything I have.

There is a current trend that a lot of travel bloggers and vloggers are promoting, which is to visit as many countries as possible, but not focusing on staying for a decent amount of time in each place to truly experience it. In contrast to this, I need to make clear that I'm an advocate for quality over quantity. In this sense, it really doesn't matter how many countries you visit, what is more important is how many quality life lessons you can learn that will make you a better person in the marathon that is life. If you don't stay long enough in one place, you won't have the opportunity to learn as much through significant experiences. I'm not saying there is no value in traveling for pleasure; it's just that focusing on longer, deeper, and more meaningful experiences will bring more noticeable improvements in your life. More bang for your buck!

When you first arrive somewhere, you'll experience the honeymoon phase where everything is magical; this is because you don't really understand what's going on yet. If you leave a country in this phase, too quickly, then you won't have as much of a chance to face any obstacles or eye-opening experiences that come with living in a place for an extended duration. It isn't until you spend a few months somewhere when you really figure out what is actually going on there. You might find that you don't really like a place as much as you did when you started, or you might like a place even more, but a decent period of time is required to truly know.

The hardest part of making this whole dream of living abroad a reality is pushing yourself to take the very first step. Beginning to read this book definitely shows you have the right intention. Now, the key will be to read until the end. It's time to take my hand, and I will guide you through the whole process very gently. Just kidding, I'm going to give you the strong shove needed to start the process of living abroad, try not to fall when I push you.

Through all of my travels, I have met hundreds, if not thousands of people from all corners of the globe who felt stuck in their lives of monotony and mediocrity. When I shared with them my life story, including my current lifestyle, I watched their eyes light up with delight. During most of these moments, I could observe their thought processes as the conversation progressed. They would initially get very excited about the lifestyle of living abroad, but then after talking more, I could see most of them hitting a mental roadblock. It was the moment they felt overwhelmed at doing it for themselves. This was the point where I would start to hear all of the excuses about why it wasn't possible for them to do it, even if it is something that they would love to pursue. I have to admit that I do enjoy hearing about people's excitement for my lifestyle, but what I truly love is helping people to realize that they too can achieve a lifestyle similar to what I have if they follow the right strategies.

A report from The Conference Board, a business research group, has found that just half of the people in the United States are satisfied with their jobs, only half! Working on something that doesn't have meaning while putting off your hopes and dreams is one of the quickest routes to a life full of regret. Life is so precious, time is running out and if we don't give it a noble purpose, then we will be left with regret, so we must seize the day!

The problem is that there so much fear of the unknown that it is challenging for many of us to let go of the perceived security that comes with a traditional job. What I want you to realize is that it's possible to build complete income security out of passive and active income that you generate for yourself. Understanding the steps to take to mitigate the risk entirely, will be able to remove the fear out of the equation, making the decision to move abroad and better your life an easy choice to make without any negative consequences.

Today, a majority of the world's work culture is set up backward. Societies around the world are encouraging their residents to overextend themselves working long hours so they can just barely be able to stay afloat financially. All of this time focused on work means sacrificing their personal dreams and freedoms in the process. If people are constantly overwhelmed with never-ending work, then how could anyone possibly have time to focus on the things that give life real purpose and value. Constantly putting off one's dreams leads to feeling empty inside. Once there is a void, most of us will practice negative behavior such as excessive shopping, excessive drinking, and other activities that only give a temporary feeling of happiness. Many of us are stuck on a hamster wheel, never able to get ahead because we are running an unfair race.

Modern work culture and work-related issues obviously vary from country to country, but this overarching trend is very apparent in each place that I have visited. To add to the list of problems, the cost of living has risen much faster than most of our incomes, making it much more stressful to just barely get by, let alone to enjoy your life.

If the system is set up for failure, then why do we even participate? Instead of finding alternatives, many people are stuck in a cycle of making a lot of money but then are forced to pay it all back for their living expenses. In this way, it is impossible to get ahead when there is no money to save after all the bills are paid. Living paycheck to paycheck is obviously not a sustainable lifestyle and will only lead to uncontrollable debt.

Another issue that only compounds the societal problem is how everyone is constantly encouraged to spend money. Everywhere we go we are bombarded with advertisements, pushing us to buy things we don't need, making it even harder to get ahead. Truth be told, we actually don't need the latest smartphone, fanciest car, or the biggest house. Overconsumption isn't making our lives better; it's making them worse by bogging us down and pulling us farther from fulfillment in life.

Most of the time, we are too busy, caught up in the rat race of life which makes it hard to see the bigger picture and realize a backward set of priorities. We are stuck in tunnel vision by a system that is designed to keep us distracted, making only the rich richer.

Living in one place only compounds the problem because we are not exposed to new ways of thinking and thus we are limited by our own minds. It's not because we are stupid, it's because we aren't getting the full education of life that is available. Living in one place only gives one side of the story of life and a very biased one at that. This would be like only watching Fox News to understand world events, what a horrible decision. It's an endless cycle that needs to be broken if we want to better ourselves and better the world as a whole. The system is built on keeping people's heads down and consuming as much as possible, without questioning why.

If you're able to realize the big picture, then you can be satisfied with knowing that there is some good news. It's completely up to us to break out of this unbalanced game that society has built and instead of competing in this psychotic rat race, we can exit and choose to pursue a life of freedom and opportunity, where we can create our own fulfillment and take control of our lifestyles. Simply being able to move to a country of your choosing and escaping an unsatisfactory situation will completely boost your quality of life and will help you to experience extreme personal development.

Living abroad has proven itself time and time again to rapidly expand a person's thinking, I've witnessed it in myself and in those around me. Life is more exciting when everything is new and there is always something to learn. Doing things in a different way than you normally do will give you a new perspective on life and what is important. This new understanding of the different ways to go about life helps give us more compassion for others and a willingness to see situations from different viewpoints. In the end, once we have grown and are better prepared mentally, we can deal with any challenge that life throws at us and crush it!

The process of personal development starts from challenging ourselves to step out of our comfort zones, into the unknown. This can be choosing not to stick to the same day-to-day habits or making a more significant impact on our growth by deciding to move to a foreign country. The life lessons learned from living abroad will ultimately make the world a much better place for all. While living abroad, the value of time is worth more because we're learning and developing much faster than if we stayed in one place. Not learning and not expanding our thinking is doing the whole world a disservice because it encourages division, fear, and violence.

Change is scary for most of us, but after you finish this book, I hope that the world will become a lot less scary. Instead of shying away from change and the unknown, I want everyone to embrace it, to learn and grow.

Like everything in life, what first appeared to be a tall and unsurpassable mountain of a challenge, becomes quite easy when broken down into manageable steps, like I do on the dance floor. This is why I created this in-depth, step-by-step guide to living abroad and thriving, so you can too develop a life of freedom and adventure that will make you wonder how you ever lived any other way.

Of course, I should warn you that just as with normal life, there will be some unpleasant parts of pushing yourself out of your comfort zone, but it's important to power through and remember that it will ultimately make you better.

If life is mediocre, then there's no reason not to

transform it into something new and exciting that brings you real fulfillment. Why accept the status quo of mediocrity and monotony when a simple move can improve your quality of life by ten times? In the famous words of Drake, "YOLO, you only live once."

Just now, another moment has passed us by that we will never get back, so let's make the most of what we have. Focusing on creating memories of incredible experiences where we learn something is what life is about. Ever since I initially made that first decision to step out of my comfort zone and begin this life of excitement, I've never wanted to go back. I'm constantly building amazing memories that I can always look back on happily and be proud to pursue meaning and not money.

How To Live Abroad and Thrive with Passive Income is divided into several parts.

> ➢ We'll begin by discussing how to choose your destination because in actuality, where you end up will ultimately dictate the quality of your experience overall.

> ➢ After the destination is chosen, I'll go into detail about the largest living expense, which is your accommodation cost, and how to find a place to live that meets your requirements.

➤ Once we have our destination and accommodations squared away, we can then calculate the overall budget for life. Having a clear plan and budget is very important because it breaks the financial component down in our minds and allows us to overcome it while putting all those pesky worries to the side. I'll also go through a series of techniques on how to save the most money and ways to make your money work for you through investing.

➤ I'll then introduce the concept of minimalism which will help to reduce stress in our lives by reducing clutter, setting our priorities so we can have the freedom to focus on what really matters in life.

➤ Then there will be the chapters on how to generate income. The first is about passive income and the second is about active income opportunities. All income streams suggested are focused on giving us freedom.

➤ Finally, I'll go into great detail on living strategies that will maximize your return on your move abroad – living life in a meaningful way while in our new foreign country, will allow us to make the most of it and thrive.

Ready to embark on an adventure of a lifetime? Are you

ready to make life as exciting as possible? Conquer each of the following chapters, and I assure you that by the end of this book, the whole process of living abroad and thriving will feel like something easy to achieve!

CHAPTER 2
THE DESTINATION

It's good that you've made the decision to move abroad. Congratulations! Now that you've decided that you want to go, you'll probably want to figure out where to go, if you don't know already. If you're risk-averse, you might have a feeling to stay in a place similar to where you're originally from. However, as you know from my introduction, the benefits of living abroad are maximized by choosing somewhere completely different than what you're familiar with. Choosing a destination too like your home country is like shooting yourself in the foot before you even start. If you don't step out of your comfort zone, then the potential for personal development will drop majorly.

If instead, you go for a place that is entirely different from where you're used to, the chance of having a significant personal development breakthrough is much higher. From my experience, I've learned that the more I step out of my comfort zone, the more challenges I overcome, the more I can learn and grow, which makes me a better and more well-rounded person. This is why there are no shortcuts in life; we are better off challenging ourselves through new experiences.

When we step into these difficult situations, it forces us to learn how to deal with new issues that arise and teaches us valuable life lessons in the process. What we learn from these new experiences makes us stronger, and thus better. The more well-rounded you become, the more you'll be able to handle any new challenges that life can throw at you. Therefore, when it comes to choosing a destination, pick a place that is insanely different than what you're used to. You can trust me on this one, I promise.

As you know, my first time living abroad was in Bangkok, Thailand. Coming from the Midwest, United States, practically every situation I encountered was brand new. I'm a very open-minded person, and relatively flexible, but this was shockingly different from my normal American life. I'll never forget that pungent sour street smell you'll occasionally get while walking around the city. Every situation I put myself in, I was forced to learn so many new things. Whether it was negotiating with street vendors, arguing with taxi drivers which is best to avoid and led to a fist fight once, crossing incredibly busy streets without getting killed, or getting used to a diverse transit system; it was all new and challenged me at every moment. Even the most mundane tasks, like getting my clothes cleaned felt magical and exciting.

The thing about Thailand was that I had no prior interest in it before arriving; I dove in head first and banged my head a few times. Even though it was new, I never felt scared at all. In hindsight, I did throw myself into a few very unsafe situations, but even in the heat of the moment, I didn't feel unsafe. That being said, avoid danger as much as possible, and remember that you are in a foreign country where you will most likely never win in an argument, especially when explaining a story to the police.

During my early days in Thailand, there was a honeymoon-phase where I enjoyed practically everything. Now that I think about it, that happy feeling about life in Thailand never really went away, even after living there for a couple of years. I remember the feeling of when I first tried tropical fruits that I had never had before, such as lychees and rambutan, my head nearly exploded from delight! There was always something new to eat! I fell in love with fish sauce with fresh chili mixed in.

I have never seen people smile so much and quickly found that unlike the United States, even poor people in

Thailand, for the most part, seemed very content with their lives. Seeing how happy they were made me rethink what is actually required for happiness. I quickly determined it's not from having tons of material possessions.

Attachment creates suffering.

People in Thailand were more laid-back than what I was used to; it made them better equipped to take on any challenges that life threw at them. I could see this when natural disasters were happening around Thailand, and the people recovered way faster than I would have expected. There was devastating damage done during flooding while I was living there, where many people's homes were destroyed. I was shocked to see that as soon as the water subsided, Thai people were quick to rebuild and get back to life, almost like nothing had ever happened. Perhaps this originates from Buddhist teachings that advocate not being attached to physical possessions.

Getting accustomed to how things worked in Thailand during day-to-day life was the easy part for me. Where it became tough was when I had to overcome barriers that I had built for myself during the twenty years of my childhood. As you know from my earlier story, when I was young, I was timid and couldn't easily talk to people. Over the years of living abroad, I've been forced into situation after situation where I had to communicate to survive. This is what I'm talking about when I say I was forced to gain confidence quickly. It worked!

Recognizing that I needed help with this, years later, while living in Hong Kong, I went above and beyond to challenge myself to approach women walking on the street to strike up conversations and get their phone numbers. Most of the time it went surprisingly well, but even when it didn't, I built my confidence with each success or denial. Nowadays, I'm not shy when I speak to absolutely anyone. It's important to remember that no matter what another person says, we don't have to take it personally, ever.

Stepping out of my comfort zone time and time again pushed me from being an introvert to thriving as an extrovert. This all originated from choosing a destination that was as different as possible than what I was accustomed to. Maybe you're not currently an introvert like I was, but rest assured that through living abroad there are unlimited ways to learn and grow.

After my semester-long exchange study program, I went back to the United States to finish out the year and a half left of my bachelor's degree. Even before I graduated, I was already planning my next trip overseas. I was infected with the travel bug. Less than one full week after I graduated from Michigan State University, I hopped on a plane and was headed to Osaka, Japan.

Long story short, my original plan for Osaka fell through, and I was forced to come up with an alternative quickly. Finding an alternative living situation in such a short time taught me a lot. I ended up emailing all the guesthouses I could find in Osaka and proposed that I trade my work for a place to stay. After receiving a few denials, I finally got one interested guesthouse. They eventually agreed and allowed me to be their English tutor in exchange for a private room.

I stayed at the guesthouse for a few months and had some amazing times where I built memories with new friends that I still fondly look back on today. Friendships I made during this time lasted for years and opened up other opportunities for me down the road. However, after living for a while in Osaka, my guesthouse living situation got a bit stressful because they had stringent, more traditional rules like not being able to bring guests to my room. With my testosterone levels peaking, that was no good for me! I often found myself daydreaming about how magical it was back in Bangkok, and eventually decided to buy a one-way ticket back.

The second time around, I encountered a whole new set of challenges than when I was a student. Now, I was operating my own business which was a whole different ball game. Instead of dealing with the common and fairly stress-free life of a student, I was now a businessman who had to acquire new clients in order to survive. I had an online marketing business at the time, and I was constantly working to build up my client list. They paid me monthly to manage their online marketing campaigns. This led to the first time in my life where I felt secure with my income. Nothing like monthly checks; more on this in the income chapters.

I lived in Bangkok for a few years and eventually moved to Hong Kong and then Seoul. Over the years to come, I repeated the process of moving to foreign countries where I didn't know anyone, and I soaked up the knowledge like a sponge in each place. Every new experience allowed me to develop personally and improve my strategies to make the whole process of moving abroad more and more efficient.

After successfully moving to several countries, I gained confidence in my methods; I can now get a new life started in a very short timeframe. That way I can hit the ground running and not break the bank or overly stress myself anywhere I end up. After nearly a decade, I learned a lot while conquering so many of my fears. I feel like there is nothing I can't overcome! It's seriously exhilarating to know that I can move anywhere in the world and survive.

That was a long introduction! It all starts with choosing the right destination for your new home. Hopefully, the one you select will introduce you to the newest experiences possible. This will give you the most room to grow. When I started, I planned less and banged my head more. However, now that I've matured, I've changed a bit, hopefully for the better, and these days I tend to consider more about a destination before I pack up my carry-on luggage and laptop bag to hop on a plane. I'll talk more about having less in the minimalism chapter!

Below are several factors to consider that I've found to be incredibly important when choosing which country to live in. Ultimately, if you have a gut feeling to move somewhere specific, I'd recommend listening to it. If not, consider the following factors to help choose your ideal country, so you don't end up in a place that makes you miserable!

Quality of Life

First and foremost, we can define the quality of life as the standard of health, comfort, and happiness experienced by an individual or a group. There are several factors that contribute to the quality of life including material living conditions, health, education, leisure and social interactions, economic and physical safety, governance and basic rights, environment, and overall experience.

Quality of life goes far beyond economics and includes standards for mental, physical, material, and social well-being. When I first moved abroad, quality of life didn't matter too much to me; I suppose I was just happy to be escaping my life in the United States. Free at last! As I've grown older and lived in several developing countries, I've realized that my quality of life standards has increased.

After living in China and Vietnam for extended periods, I learned how bad air pollution could be. The thing about air pollution is that looks can be deceiving. Some days, even with the bluest of blue skies, there can be very high air pollution. It was so bad that I often had to plan the times that I would exercise outdoors based around when the pollution wasn't too unhealthy.

PM 2.5 refers to atmospheric particulate matter that has a diameter of less than 2.5 μm. These particles are so small that they tend to stay in the air longer which increases the chance of inhaling them. These particles can bypass our natural filters of the nose and throat and go far deeper and get stuck in our lungs. Studies have found a close link between exposure to these fine particles and premature death from heart and lung disease. Sounds pleasant right?

I've also learned that when the level of PM 2.5 exceeds 160, there is more harm in exercising outdoor for 30 minutes then skipping the work out altogether. Air pollution is disgusting and something I learned that I'm not willing to live with for long periods. I'm drawn to countries like China and India, but I don't want to put my long-term health in jeopardy. So, I will adjust my plans accordingly. It's so sad.

On the contrary, one of the cleanest countries I've lived in has been Japan. Opposed to popular belief, I have found Japan to be very affordable and offer a seriously great quality of life. There's so much value for your money, especially when it comes to tasty food!

There are many features that I appreciate about Japan which include its affordable and convenient public transportation, high level of healthcare, cleanliness, a warm culture, lots of green space, well maintained public facilities including having public toilets everywhere, advanced infrastructure, great education system, very low crime rate, high-standards for food quality, clean drinking water, and all the political freedoms most Western democracies share. I must say it does give me a great sense of peace to be in Japan. I seldom have to worry about my safety there. Before Japan, I have always lived in countries with much higher crime rates where you always have to be concerned about criminals. Living in Japan is a dream!

Overall, as we travel and live abroad, we can see that the world tends to be way safer than what the news may make it seem. That being said, some places are dangerous, such as war-torn countries, areas with high crime rates, or countries with lots of terrorism that I would simply avoid. I'm generally an advocate for pushing the limits, but this is where I draw the line.

There is no need to risk your life just for a thrill. Please use your common sense; I don't need any lawsuits.

A lot of safety concerns will come down to your situational awareness. If you are aware of your surroundings, then it will generally be tough for someone to take advantage of you. Notice the little things and how people are moving around, keeping your eyes open for something suspicious. My head is always on a swivel, if not for crime, for avoiding accidents. Things happen fast, and if you're not in the moment, you will suffer. Put the phone away and focus!

Ultimately, the quality of life you're willing to accept is up to your personal preferences. There's no way I can tell you exactly what is best for you. Do you like it dirty? I have found my preference through experience, which I feel is the best option for most people. It's easy to say you don't like something, but if you haven't experienced it, how can you know for sure? I can say that when I was younger, I preferred developing countries, regardless of the quality of living as they tended to be more exciting. Everything moves so quickly!

Cost of Living

It's easy to find data online that ranks countries in order of cost of living. Regardless of this information, I've been able to control my cost of living and keep it fairly consistent in all of the countries I've lived or visited. Whether they are known for being expensive or affordable, I find that if I'm comparing the same quality of something, such as food, the costs tend to be quite similar worldwide. If you are willing to lower your standards for quality, then it is possible to make things much cheaper.

For example, you can eat street food in developing countries, and it will be dirt cheap and probably tasty, but in the process of saving money, you'll be sacrificing sanitation levels, food quality, and you have no idea where it came from. Another example would come with renting or buying housing. It's entirely possible to live in a developing country such as China for bargain prices. However, the building might literally fall apart after a short period.

In life, you get what you pay for.

On the contrary, in wealthier countries where everything seems to be more expensive, there are creative ways to keep costs down, which I will discuss in greater depth in the savings chapter. The cost of living will ultimately come down to your own frugality and not merely what the data dictates. From my experience, I found that there are always deals to be had, regardless of the country, if you know where to look. Accommodation cost tends to be the highest living expense in all countries. Other things to consider about the cost of living are income taxes and how much this will put a burden on your life.

Working Environment

Different countries have different working cultures and environments. How your working life will be will significantly depend on if you choose to work for yourself or someone else. I completely understand that not everyone wants to be an entrepreneur; some people just feel better with the benefits and a steady paycheck from an employer. Having different types of people in this world is what makes it special.

The working culture in the United States is generally fairly straightforward. People usually go to work for designated work hours, and that's that. In Japan, it is quite different, as I met lots of people who work until late at night. It seems more unknown when they will finish because there's always so much to do, and it all depends greatly on the personality of their boss. Of course, I'm not saying every company is the same everywhere, just investigate the working culture in the place that you are going to before you accept a job offer there.

If you do go the job route, I recommend doing something that excites you and that will teach you about the place you're living. If you are interested in working for yourself, then read on to explore passive and active income ideas coming in later chapters.

Visa Requirements

Another huge factor when choosing a destination will come down to the visa requirements. As I meet more and more people, I have learned just how big of a role a person's passport can play in determining where they can go and how long they can stay. Learning that you can't go somewhere because of where you were born can be super depressing.

I came to this brutal realization when dating past girlfriends. A lot of the countries that I didn't even have to consider needing a visa for would require them to get one. Then to obtain said visa would require lots of documents, needless hurdles, and high visa fee payments. Luckily somehow, they would always get approved for our travels, but not without added cost, hassle, and stress.

If you are unfortunate enough to have a weak passport that doesn't allow you to go to many countries, don't worry, your life isn't over, and the chances of living abroad aren't ruined, but this is sadly something you'll need to consider when choosing your destination. If your passport is too restrictive, I would recommend getting a second citizenship if possible. For me, getting a second citizenship is a fantasy, while for others, it may be a necessity if they want to see more of the world. Damn the world!

Up until this point in my life living around the world, I've never needed to acquire a work visa. This is because I've always worked for myself, and a majority of my income has come through the United States, which is my legal country of residence. For nearly a decade, I've been living abroad exclusively on tourist visas or staying in countries with visa exemptions.

To stay for an extended period, I would simply utilize a visa-run strategy. This doesn't require jogging, don't worry! Visa runs entail exiting a country before your time limit on your visa expires and then re-entering to reset the clock and stay for another duration of time. For example, as an American, there are several countries that I can visit visa-free, and am granted 90 days upon arrival. To stay longer than the 90 days I would simply leave the country, and then return after taking a trip, where I'd be granted another 90 days. Boom 180 days, or boom unlimited days!

Some countries do restrict the amount of time you can spend there per year on a tourist visa, so you'll have to do your homework before knowing if this will work for your situation. Ultimately, this will depend on your individual passport requirements.

With the rise in popularity of living and working abroad, I've read that some countries are offering special visas for Digital Nomads. I would look into other creative visa options if you're looking to stay in one country for an extended period without having to leave.

Climate

Growing up in the Midwest of the United States, I was very familiar with frigid weather and grey skies. Oftentimes, when I was younger, we would get tons and tons of snow and have frigid winters, less so these days. Summers were usually very comfortable, not normally getting super hot. As I got older, I realized that I wanted to enjoy warm climates more. Warm just wasn't something I got to experience a lot while growing up. What can I say, I like it hot!

As an adult, I have focused on countries that have tropical weather. Over time, my preference has shifted back and forth between enjoying cold and hot weather. I'm not sure why people make such a big deal about the weather, because no matter if the climate is hot or cold, a majority of countries have systems in place to keep people comfortable. For example, if you're in the Middle East, you will constantly be going from one air-conditioned space to another. If you are in a cold place, then you will constantly be going from one heated space to another. I think sometimes people make too big of a deal about climate when deciding where to go. At the end of the day, if you are prepared with the correct clothing, you can be comfortable wherever you end up.

The two largest factors to consider when choosing your

destination will ultimately come down to the cost of living and your passport requirements. If your passport doesn't allow you to go somewhere, then the only solution would be to find a creative visa solution or to get a new passport. I would ultimately advise everyone to choose a country that offers an extremely different culture then what you're already familiar with, especially while you're young. The greater the change in culture, the more challenges you will overcome, and the more you will learn and grow. Once you've experienced a few challenging countries, down the line, you might want to take the route of somewhere more developed and convenient, but it's all up to you.

CHAPTER 3
ACCOMMODATION

As I've mentioned, way too many times, the highest living expense, no matter where in the world we live, is usually the cost of accommodation. Now that you've chosen your destination, hopefully somewhere very different than what you're used to, it is time to consider where you will live while there. Just as with deciding which country to visit, choosing where you will live while at your destination is incredibly important and will have real influence on how much you get out of your living abroad experience.

I recognized how hefty the accommodation cost could be early on, and for the last ten years, I've focused on living situations that are either free, bartered for work, or as affordable as possible. Currently, half of my year involves me staying and working with hotels which I don't have to pay out-of-pocket for, and the other half I'm either visiting family members or paying a modest rent. If you're wondering, and I know you are, the way my blog works is that I will offer media coverage in exchange for luxury accommodation and high-end food. My media coverage comes in the form of articles and social media posts which I will publish on my website and social media channels. The longest collaboration stay I ever had was 11 nights! What a good memory in Shanghai. Not only did I have 11 nights, but the stay also came with club lounge access. For this hotel, it meant that I had three meals a day. You can't make this stuff up!

If I'm paying for everything including all living expenses, my spending typically never exceeds $1,500 a month, no matter what country I'm living in. I understand this is not possible for everyone in every country, but if you work hard at finding a deal on your accommodation, the possibility of keeping your overall expenses down greatly increases.

For me, if we consider that I only require six months of rent per year, I will save $9,000 because half of my accommodation for the year is provided. It's really easy to see how this can add up over time and immensely boost my savings rate. Long story short, because I won't bore you with how amazing my life is, I get to enjoy a luxury lifestyle in exchange for my very valuable services. Bartering becomes an option when you have something of value to offer in exchange for what you are seeking.

Nevermind, I'll share just one example! On a recent trip to the United Arab Emirates, where I stayed for a full month, two weeks in Dubai and two weeks in Abu Dhabi, I only spent $100 out of my pocket for two people. If this doesn't get you excited, I don't know what will! I'm all giddy just reminiscing.

For the other six months out of the year, I live the peasant lifestyle like everybody else. Joking, I've always lived quite well, even before my blogging days. I focused on making my money go the farthest as possible while I lived in foreign countries.

Accommodation should never be left until the last minute, as it often requires lots of research to find a real diamond in the rough deal. If you don't plan well, accommodation costs can ultimately break you and your time abroad. You don't want to be stuck at home all the time eating rice and drinking water because you chose an apartment that was too expensive. Once you organize an affordable accommodation, the requirement for your monthly income will be much easier to reach. When your rent is low, you'll have less stress to earn money and have more free time to focus on what's important in your life. Don't bite off more than you can chew with an expensive apartment. Once you feel comfortable paying your rent, only then should you consider paying more for a different place. Jumping into a place that is too expensive too fast can completely disrupt your life; be careful.

If you're moving to a city, it's important to consider a few things while deciding where in that city to live. I would generally recommend living near the things that you enjoy, or if you require a job, then not too far away from your employer. Being near public transportation is very important as well, as it will greatly impact your monthly expenses.

Something to consider is that as you go farther away from a city's center, the rent will be lower, but transportation costs will increase. Perhaps that amazingly cheap rent won't be worth it if you require an expensive and long commute every day. In some cases, it might be more worthwhile, considering both time and money, to pay more in rent, and live right in the city's center with low transportation costs. This has been something I've had to juggle time and time again. Ultimately, I will always choose a more convenient location, amid all the action, over a long commute any day of the week. I like to stay where lots of food is located, and being more centrally located makes it convenient to set a meeting point near where you live when going on dates or meeting friends.

In every city I've visited, there usually tends to be an area with a higher percentage of foreigners. Stay away!

As opposed to the popular belief of many expats, I would recommend avoiding living near foreigners, and instead, living in a community that is filled to the brim with locals. If you're going to leave your own country to live abroad, there's no sense in living near people that are the same as where you just came from. Time and time again, I've witnessed swaths of foreigners sticking together to form a foreign bubble and not truly learning about the foreign culture that they are living in. It's seriously depressing. Let's be wise.

This being said, allow me to share a small word of caution from my past living experiences. While living in Shenzhen, China, I lived in an extremely "local" residential area. It was one of the older parts of the city where you would practically never see foreigners. Over time, it ended up being a little hard to take, because Chinese culture is so, intense, for lack of better words.

Looking at the bright side, the benefit of living in such a local area is that it will take you out of your comfort zone, forcing you to learn and adapt while making you a better person. This might be fine for a shorter period of time, but we should consider how we will feel over months and months. We can still learn a lot and not kill ourselves in the process. Looking back on that time, I still believe it was a very positive experience, even though it was a bit hard to digest at times.

I realized I can't just talk about these rough parts of

Chinese culture vaguely. Some examples included living near a family who had children that were constantly screaming like they were being butchered; near the metro station by my place I witnessed children peeing on the floor, multiple times; everywhere I went in my area I was stared at very intensely; people constantly spitting, burping, and farting, but this is hard to avoid in most of China. This list can go on and on, but the moral of the story is that living in an environment where everything is constantly wearing on you can be tough in the long-run. Balance.

Over my three years in Thailand, I basically lived in just two areas in Bangkok. The first area was near Chulalongkorn University, which is where I studied, in an area known as Siam. It was a great place to get my first foreign living experience going, and very convenient as it was close to school, restaurants, public transportation, and lots of ladies; I was 20!

When I returned for my second time living in Bangkok, I ended up living in the Thonglor area, which if you didn't know, is an area mixed with residential, restaurants, and lots of nightlife. Thonglor is also known for being expensive, but the entire time I lived there, for about two years, I found it very affordable, as I kept finding deals on my accommodation. Thonglor really fit my lifestyle perfectly at the time, because I was in my mid-20s and enjoyed such a lively area. My apartment was also near the Thonglor BTS station, which is Bangkok's elevated train. Being near the train allowed me to get around the rest of the city quickly and easily. During my time living there, I never spent more than $500 a month for my accommodation; this left me $500-$1,000 of my budget to use for mostly eating and fun! Trust me, a lot can be had in Thailand for $500-$1,000 a month.

When searching for accommodation, it can be challenging to sift through all of the garbage listings out there that are full of inflated prices. Back when I started my search in Bangkok, there were tons of listings on popular English websites such as Craigslist and Facebook. Although these looked like decent prices compared to developed countries, compared to local prices, they were nearly double, buyer beware.

Lucky for you, this is now no longer the case in Bangkok, as real estate has become more mainstream with websites in both English and Thai languages. However, this lesson I learned taught me to confirm that we really have to be careful when it comes to finding accommodation. This is an example of how large of a role using the right search method can impact the price and ultimately our quality of life we experience while abroad.

For this reason, it is essential to compare the rental listings that you have found with what a local would actually pay. This may take searching for websites that aren't in English, or simply asking locals their opinion if it is a good value or not. The more people you can ask, the better. Knowing the local language might help in this case, but Google Translate can translate any foreign language website.

The apartment that I found in Bangkok from searching Thai real estate websites had everything I needed all for around $450 a month including utilities! It was in Thonglor, which was a high-end area of Bangkok, and included a kitchen, pool, gym, washing machine, sauna, shuttle to the nearest station, and 24/7 security. It was near the end of a quiet street that was very peaceful but nearby everything I wanted.

Nowadays I guarantee that you would pay around double if you found a comparable apartment in the area on an English only website. If you consider the $400-$500 of savings per month because I took the time to find a great deal, it's easy to see how quickly that can add up over the year and greatly impact lifestyle. This could be up to a $6,000 savings. This is why it is so important to put in the time searching to make sure you're finding a real deal and not wasting money on an inflated price.

Several types of accommodation come with different price points and features. In my early days, I began with shared accommodations. Especially if you're completely new to a country, I recommend this as its the cheapest way to go, as well as it is an option that will help introduce you to lots of other people allowing you to grow your network rapidly. Some of my best friends came from the time that I lived together with them in a sharehouse at Michigan State University. Everyone, of course, starts as a stranger, and then you become more like a family.

By living together, a group can't help but go through experiences that will bond them together. This bonding tends to build lasting friendships. If you don't know anyone, this can be a great jumping off point to get your networking going, especially if your housemates have already been there for a while. They can introduce you to their friends, and then your circle will expand.

Generally, sharing a house will reduce your rental expense by about half making it a very cost-effective way to live. There are some downsides including lack of privacy, no walking around naked, but you should be able to find a place that's suitable for your requirements. Even after I decided not to do accommodation sharing at a point in my life, I changed my mind because in Japan I just couldn't pass up the amazing deal. In 2019 I paid $550 a month for a room in a shared house that had a kitchen and was very modern. There was no deposit and no contract, just a minimum of a 30-day stay. The culture plays a big role in this because the way it was set up works great in Japan where people are mostly respectful of others.

The share house was similar to a serviced apartment

because it was cleaned regularly by the staff. They also supplied quite a bit including appliances, food supplies, cleaning supplies, and bedding. Housemates respected me and kept quiet all the time which was very nice. In Korea and Japan, they have share houses which work quite well, but I honestly doubt this level of peace would be achieved in other countries. In the share house, I lived at in university, it was a completely different story.

At the end of the day, my first choice when it comes to choosing a style of accommodation is still private. Once you've lived somewhere with people and gained knowledge of the city and have your life more figured out, it will be possible to switch to private accommodation. It may be slightly more expensive, but if you're someone like me, who likes things done in a certain way, you might feel more content with your own space.

While in Korea, I lived in the Apgujeong neighborhood which is one of the higher income areas in Seoul. The cost of real estate was very high, but it was a popular place to hang out among my age group, so I rarely had to travel anywhere to meet people because they all were happy to come to where I lived. Living in Apgujeong allowed me to be around great food and people all the time. I was only a couple hundred meters from the nearest metro stations. My apartment was also near the Han River which was a great place to exercise all year round. In the summertime, it became a great hangout spot as well. I have so many fond memories of ordering delivery fried chicken directly to the riverside to enjoy with a beer and good company. My apartment wasn't even close to luxury, but for the price of $650, all included was impossible to pass up. My studio apartment was equipped with a full kitchen, bed with bedding, wifi, and television. The bare essentials but it worked for me because the convenience trumped all.

Everyone's requirements will be slightly different when it comes to choosing accommodation. As I'll mention later in the savings chapter, kitchens will be very important for those who are budget conscious because allowing yourself to cook your own food saves you tons of cash. I also value a convenient location, even if you have to pay a little bit more. When it comes to the price, I generally like to spend between $500 in $1000 a month. This rent might not be 100% possible in every major city, but it should be possible in most places.

At the end of the day, the major points are that it's probably not worth living farther away from the city center because it will be harder to get things done including meeting people and exploring the popular areas of the city. While living in the city's center, you won't be spending a lot on transportation which will always help. Don't throw away money by not finding the best deal. Be sure to look for rentals where the locals look and ask for a local person's opinion on what you find. In the beginning, I would recommend a shared living situation, but once you establish yourself, you might want to consider moving to your own place. Finding a deal on accommodation is super important!

CHAPTER 4
BUDGET AND SAVING

One of the biggest pieces of the puzzle of living abroad, which I often get asked about, is how to manage it financially. For my lifestyle, a huge component has been my ability to save money and make my money work for me. I learned that how you save is just as valuable, if not more valuable, than how much you earn. This is because it doesn't matter how much you earn if you can't save anything.

From day one, frugality has been the basis of my success. From a young age, I was taught the difference between a need and a want. I do occasionally splurge on myself, very occasionally, but overall I just tend to be happiest with having less. When it's possible to reduce spending and increase saving it gives more wiggle room when it comes to how much income is required to meet our monthly requirements.

In the beginning, when you first move, this can be very important if you don't have work already lined up for yourself. If you are able to save enough money, then you will feel a lot more at ease and have less pressure to find income. The period of little or no income might be unknown upon your arrival if you're looking for jobs. Unless you have your own business and you already have income coming in, then there could be a month or two, or maybe more without any income and we need to plan ahead and prepare for this.

This is the time when it's important to already have savings and be frugal so you can make those savings last for as long as possible while you figure out what you need to do. The data suggests that a large portion of people don't have much savings and are sadly living paycheck to paycheck. It would be tough to move abroad and not have any savings to support your new lifestyle. If you don't plan properly, you may be forced to return to your home country quicker than expected, while not being able to get anything out of the experience so listen up. This chapter will outline the mindset and strategies required to make your money go as far as possible while you are living abroad or just living in general. All strategies are designed to reduce financial hardship and stress so you can focus more on what's important in life and less on earning money.

Lucky for me, from a young age, my parents taught me how to save. They made me work for my money and showed me that I didn't always need to spend it to have a good time. I would mostly save up to buy my latest toys; I started with Legos and worked my way up to cars. My mother was a huge bargain shopper, and my dad was an entrepreneur, so between the two of them, I learned a great deal about financial responsibility. It's still ingrained in my mind about hunting for bargains from my mom and working for myself from my dad that still sticks with me to this day.

When I was just nine years old, I started my own candy selling business, and business was booming from the start! I still fondly remember the time I sold one piece of candy to a kid for five dollars. I hustled him so hard. Don't be mad; I was just a kid! From then until now I've had dozens and dozens of incomes including part-time jobs and many of my own businesses which include when I was 16 with my online shoe and apparel store where I imported my stock directly from China; a t-shirt business where I designed and sold hundreds of shirts; clearing tables at a fine dining restaurant where I earned $30 per hour also at age 16; a website design business that I had for about a decade; when I was a professional photographer and videographer producing music videos, wedding videos, fashion photoshoots, commercial, and basically anything someone would pay me for; an online marketing business where I had several clients paying me monthly; when I was a professional music producer for a short time I made and sold hip-hop beats; an Internet reselling business where I bought used items and resold them online for a profit; became a full-time food and travel writer; most recently where I've become a real estate investor and the list goes on. Basically, I've done everything under the sun to earn money while younger and then as I grew up, honing my skills on what I feel passionate about.

Throughout my life, there was always a common theme of saving more than I spent. No matter what you're doing in life, this is a very important strategy for obvious reasons. As far as I'm concerned, there's never a point to spending more than you earn and getting yourself into debt. Even now I compare my adult friends who are sometimes making ten times more income than I am, but they're also only able to save a small fraction of what they earn. Often times, I am able to save what they save or more, and this just shows how important it is to be frugal, especially when income is low. Time and time again it's easy to witness people blowing the money they've made and have nothing to show for it; what a mistake. Not only should we be able to save but we also need to make our money work for us, and it will grow exponentially.

First things first, let's calculate our requirements for our living expenses. As mentioned in the last chapter, accommodation will be your largest living expense no matter if you're living abroad or not. Now that you have done your research and know where you want to live, note down the price of potential accommodations options. Simply noting a range of rental fees is acceptable. For me, as I mentioned before, I generally spend between $500 and $1,000 a month on my rental costs.

The next thing we need to add to the list of our monthly expenses is food. Food costs vary depending on what and where you're eating. Overall, buying raw ingredients and cooking your food will be better for your health and your pocketbook. Even if you think you're a lousy chef now, anyone can follow a recipe. Cooking will make your money stretch, and if you need to lose weight, you can restrict your calories as well to save even more. On a recent period of intense savings after tiding myself over before new rental incomes came in, I began skipping breakfast and got down to my ideal weight!

I highly recommended cooking whether it's for financial reasons or because it makes us more independent and ultimately a better person. Eating out at restaurants, especially in countries like the United States, where food prices are so inflated, it's just not worth it not to cook. Even if you're spending on the lower end while eating out, let's say you spend $10 per meal, that adds up to roughly $30 per day. If instead, you take $30 that might last you for 3-4 days if you buy raw ingredients and cook your own food. In my opinion, once you or your partner is good at cooking, you can have just as good of, if not a better, experience eating at home than eating at a restaurant. I find it really enjoyable to plan and prepare an amazing meal.

Like I mentioned, I prepare and eat most of my meals at home. I'll ignore the fact that I'm basically only having two meals a day because not everyone will be like me. Let's go through my food expenditures in Tokyo, which is supposedly one of the most expensive cities in the world. For breakfast, I normally have two eggs, fried potatoes, a banana, and a cup of coffee which would cost $1.75 total. For lunch let's say I cooked fried chicken, rice, and a salad which would be about $3.00-$4.50 depending on what you add. For dinner, I buy something like wagyu or sashimi and have it with some rice, vegetables, and sake which would be around $7-$9 because I really like to enjoy my life. Wink. The total for this one day on the high end would cost $15.25 and for the month would be $457.50. I'm often skipping a meal and also often make my dinner costs less but because I wanted to give a higher-end example in case you too also like to live! It's always better to overestimate your expenses instead of underestimating them.

Transportation costs are another important expense to consider. If you want to be healthy and save the most money, walking is the best. Public transportation is usually the next cheapest option after walking for free. Once you switch to taxis, the fees generally are quite a bit more unless you're in a developing country. In Southeast Asia, public transport costs are quite economical and tend to be clean and safe modes of transportation. You'll have to weigh your individual options to see what works best for you. Now it is time to calculate roughly how much you think you'll spend per month on transportation. For me in Tokyo, I only need to take public transportation 2-3 times a week which roughly costs me $50 a month.

Additional miscellaneous costs such as entertainment costs are bigger for some people than others. For me, the only real entertainment costs I have is going out to eat and drink which mostly fits into the food category. I don't spend much on other things, so this would come down to what your personal preferences are. What do you like to do in your free time? Perhaps Netflix, going to a movie, whatever it is that you entertain yourself with. For myself, I'll add another $100 a month just to be on the safe side.

Now, be sure to add up all of your monthly expenses and to find your total. I'm sure some things apply to you and some don't, so be sure to add or subtract those as well. The main reason it's important to overestimate this number is that you don't want to come up short for planning how much income you will need to make. As an example, for my current lifestyle in Tokyo, my rent including utilities is $550, my food is $457.50, transportation $50, and miscellaneous are $100 for a grand total of $1,157.50 in living expenses per month.

In my mind, I always estimate my monthly budget somewhere between $1,000 and $1,500. Even though we know my real expenditures, we can just round up and assume they are $1,500 a month to be safe for any unplanned expenses. I've had great comfort in knowing that my passive income can cover these costs already. Don't worry, all my passive income details are coming up in the passive income chapter!

At the end of the day, knowing my budget and the fact that it's covered by income I don't actively have to work for gives me a great deal of security and allows me to have free time to focus on my passion projects. Bow chica wow wow.

Now that you have added up all your living expenses for the month, next let's calculate how much savings we will need to generate before we can make our move abroad comfortably and stress-free. Personally, I'd like to build up a safety net of six months to one year of savings which you can live on if you have zero money coming in. For me, six months would require $9,000, and one year would require $18,000 for living expenses. I rarely ever watch my savings decrease but having the safety net just brings a sense of security. Hopefully, you already have this in your bank account, if not, follow my saving and investing strategies below! Don't skimp on your savings because if you do and you run into an emergency, you will simply be stuck with no easy way out, unless you have a rich uncle. Joking, let's never depend on others financially again!

Now that we have a budget squared away, it's time to discuss saving strategies. The theme of saving should be all about maintaining a slow and steady growth rate. When we rush or get greedy, the chance of losing everything increases significantly. Knowing your monthly expenditure requirements along with calculating your savings requirements will be helpful for the rest of your master plan. When we have a goal to achieve, it will be much easier to reach it instead of some arbitrary number. Even writing this makes me feel at peace. Until we make a plan for conquering these obstacles such as living expenses, we can easily make them way more difficult than they need to be which makes things feel overwhelming, and that's no fun. Once we identify the problem, find a solution, and then create a plan with smaller steps, everything becomes possible to overcome.

Now let's go through financial strategies which will help you attain your new budget goals for reducing monthly expenditures and building your savings.

Track Income and Expenditures

The first strategy that I use is tracking all of my income and expenditures. I've been using a free online tool accessible both by website and app called Mint, by the brand Intuit. It's possible to link credit cards, investments, bank accounts, loans, and bills to Mint which allows us to see all inflows and outflows of money in one place. I can see my net worth over time and a real-time amount of how much I have after credit card balances. Now I rarely ever have to log in to each individual bank account or credit card to see my information. There are multiple services out there that can do this, but this has worked well for me. No matter what tool you use, make sure that it only has read-only access to your information. Mint has no ability to make changes to any of my accounts, so even if a hacker gained access, they could only see my information but not details such as account information.

Tracking income and expenditures helps me see exactly where I'm spending and making money so I can see right away if there are any issues to take note of. If you're constantly tracking your finances, it's harder to make mistakes from ignorance. Since all of my transactions are tracked, this also works well during tax time when I have to report all of my financial information. I am in no way receiving anything from Intuit for my recommendation, although I wish I was! I also use their TurboTax product for doing my own taxes.

Asset Liquidation

Another way to save is by selling things that still have

value that you don't need anymore. If you're like most people, you've built up quite a collection of stuff over the years. Now that you've decided to move abroad, get rid of all those things and earn some cash to build your savings account. Go through all items and ask yourself if you will truly need it while living your life abroad. I get by just fine with my single carry on luggage.

If you haven't used something in six months, you probably don't need it at all. Once you get rid of your unused things, I guarantee you'll feel lighter and have an increased sense of freedom; I'll talk more about that in the minimalism chapter. I have experience selling my items on Facebook, Craigslist, and eBay. Facebook and Craigslist are nice because there are currently no listing or fees associated with selling; let's hope that doesn't change in the future. Unfortunately, eBay does charge fairly substantial fees plus you have to ship the items. For items that you can't sell, I would recommend donating them to people in need. Remember to meet people in public places such as a cafe when selling your items for your safety and donate to real charities, not for profit organizations with ulterior motives.

Buy Generic

There are cheaper alternatives for nearly everything you buy. Lots of the time, products of the exact same quality are available as the more expensive ones; the only difference is the lack of a brand name. We have been programmed our entire lives to buy new and to buy the brand names when we need something. Sometimes, the well-known brand name is the best quality for the price, but many times, when it's not, go for the generic version. For example, I tailor my suits in Bangkok instead of buying name brands at the store. I only spend about 30% of the price of a big fashion brand, and I get a better fit because it is tailored just for little old me. Just because it's branded doesn't mean it's any better.

Buy Second-Hand

Even though we have a knee-jerk reaction to doing something, doesn't mean it's always necessary. Does that coffee machine that you just bought really need to be brand-new or can you search on Facebook or Craigslist and find a used one for half the price? Buying second-hand is great for the environment because it creates less waste and saves tons of money. Buying many bigger ticket items new doesn't have an upside. For example, when you buy a new car, within the first year, the car will lose 20% of its value on average.

Make It Last, Skip the Latest Version

If you have something that gets the job done and there is no real push to upgrade, then there isn't a lot of value in buying the latest version as soon as it comes out. We are always programmed by the latest of everything, but in reality, it just doesn't improve our lives that much. Don't get caught up with all the other sheep; if you've got something that works, make it last until it doesn't anymore. For example, I have been using the same point and shoot camera for four years. It's very common for photographers to get caught up in buying more and more equipment, but at the end of the day, it's the eye of the photographer that ultimately makes the picture, not the camera or lens. The same thing goes with my phone and laptop, which I have made last for at least a few new product release cycles. Be happy with what you have; more on this later.

Miles Travel

Another great way to save money that I've utilized a ton over the years is by booking my airfare with airline miles. Ever since I started traveling solo about ten years ago, I watched airline ticket prices fall. Back when I started, flights were nearly double what they cost today. Good news for us! Back then, because flights were so expensive, I researched for cheaper alternatives and eventually discovered the beauty of airline miles.

There has always been a wide variety of airline miles schemes available. From my experience, the most bang for your buck will come from signing up for credit cards that offer airline mile bonuses upon meeting spending requirements. Usually the spending requirement is around $3,000 or more, and then customers receive about $500 in rewards. Most of the time, the bonus worked out to a one-way, long-haul flight from my experience. For me, this would either be a one-way flight to Asia from Chicago or vice versa.

If you pay off your credit card balance in full and on time every month, you will have nothing else to worry about. You will get rewarded by spending money like you normally would anyways! The minute you fall behind is when the credit card companies win, and this must happen enough to make it all worthwhile. Over the years, I was able to get 1-2 long-haul flights paid for by miles each year for the last ten years. All these reward flights saved me between $7,000 and $12,000. That's all from spending like I normally would but strategizing, so I could get the airline mile bonuses.

Since I'm so frugal, I often didn't have a lot of purchases to make, so I would plan to make big purchases according to when I got the credit cards. That way, I never struggled to meet the spending requirements to get the bonuses. These bonuses are constantly changing, and some of the credit cards do come along with yearly membership fees. Most of the annual membership fees don't go over $125. In the past, I was able to call customer service before it was time to renew and asked if they would remove the yearly fee; this has worked a few times in the past years.

Nowadays, if the credit card company refuses to remove the fee, I will generally cancel the card. There are occasions where it is better to pay the fee if you are constantly out of the country like me because the alternative would be cards that have foreign transaction fees that would quickly add up to much more than the $100 a year for the better reward credit card.

The greatest part is that many of these rewards can be redeemed again and again through the process of churning. Churning credit cards simply means getting the deal again by following the credit card company's guidelines. All have different requirements for how long you have to wait before getting another card from the same company and also usually a rule about how many cards you can have simultaneously.

Unfortunately, all of this churning of credit cards has finally caught up with me after ten years of pillaging the rewards like a greedy pirate! Now, I've got to wait to apply for new cards because I've reached a limit by some of the major card companies. I should be able to get back at it again in another six months to a year. Keep in mind that to qualify for these cards in the first place requires a great credit score, so if you don't have one, start with more basic credit cards and build your credit score. These rewards credit cards generally offer additional bonuses in addition to the sign-up bonus such as preferential boarding, free baggage, or airline lounge access.

If I would have considered the rules of the cards in

advance, I probably wouldn't even have to take a break from continually churning these credit card bonus deals. However, since I went in without an initial plan, I shot myself in the foot and now have to sit on the sidelines for a little while. If you take the time to look up the rules for each credit card, you could plan out when you will sign up for each one so you can rotate them in a way that meets all of the guidelines for the different companies and not make the same mistake I did. All in all, this is a great way to get free, or nearly free, long-haul flights.

Let the Bank Work for You

Saving on banking fees can have a huge impact on your monthly expenditures while living abroad. Most people don't realize how many fees are associated with banks. The main one while abroad is either international transaction fees or ATM fees. I'm not affiliated with Charles Schwab, but I have had great success with them over the years. They completely reimburse all ATM fees! To be clear, the reimbursable ATM fees aren't just in the United States but are worldwide.

This means that you'll never have to exchange money again! Simply go to an ATM in whatever country you're in and withdraw money at the exact market exchange rate that is currently available all with no additional fees. You won't have to hold onto extra cash that could be stolen or lost, just take out what you need and get reimbursed for the ATM fees later. This has been so convenient for my lifestyle abroad and led to saving thousands and thousands of dollars over the years. My ATM transaction fees add up to at least $25 a month just to withdraw money. You can thank me later!

Eliminate Monthly Expenditures

Another great way to save money is by looking for alternatives to monthly expenses. There are many monthly expenses out there that quickly add up that most of us don't even think about. If we analyze how much we are actually spending and on what, we can look for cheaper or free alternatives.

Exercise for Free

For example, having an expensive gym membership is a good way to spend a lot of money and maybe not see a lot of results. First of all, let's stop the all too common trend of working out just for our looks, it isn't healthy. Exercising should simply be for our health. This fitness trend on social media has gotten out of hand and turned into a way for insecure people to try and fill a void within them with a temporary superficial fix. Don't get me wrong, exercising is great, but we should be doing it for the right reasons. Changing the purpose of working out to focus on our health and building our confidence through other means, will make a gym membership unneeded.

To be healthy, all you do is build your strength and endurance through activities such as jogging, biking, and bodyweight exercises. A great workout can occur in a public park and doesn't require spending hundreds of dollars a month for a gym membership. Save the roughly $1,200 a year and use the money on a flight and workout for free. Along with eating well to stay my optimum body weight, I also run outside a few times a week and do push-ups, pull-ups, an ab workout, squats, and am in great physical condition because of it; it doesn't require any additional money.

Make Drinking Cheaper

Alcohol consumption is another way that we can quickly throw our money away. Going out for drinks is a costly activity, especially over time. Not only is alcohol bad for our health, but can also be a train wreck for your pocketbook. Ever look at what you spent on a night out and consider all the other ways you could use that money?

When you consider the cost of a drink at an establishment versus buying the bottle at the store, it just doesn't make sense to be paying so much for the same thing. Learning how to make drinks yourself at home or finding a cheaper place can be great alternatives compared to the high-priced bar you always get drunk at. This won't be entirely accurate, because it will depend on what you drink, but let's just assume that it costs you roughly $2 to make your favorite drink at home, and that same drink costs $10 at the bar. If you drank one drink a day for a month and made your own, it would cost $60, compared with costing $300 at the bar!

At the end of the day, it's about who you are with not the surroundings. When I was younger, I was into going out to the clubs. After enjoying clubbing for a few years, I'd be out drinking at my favorite clubs and realized that we were all standing in a big dirty room with the lights off while paying a premium for drinking basic drinks we could enjoy anywhere. Granted there are some exceptional venues that we can treat ourselves to on occasion, but moderation is key.

I absolutely love buying my favorite drink at the store and then going to a beautiful public space such as a river, lake, or park and enjoying it there. Many times the only thing separating an outdoor bar is a fence. Why pay the premium to stand inside the fence versus outside?

Skip the Cafe

Buying coffee at a cafe is a similar concept to buying drinks at a bar but possibly worse. When you consider the actual cost of making coffee yourself at $.25 a cup and compare it to the $3 you'd spend at a cafe, the 12 times markup is really quite incredible. It's even scarier when you consider the total cost for a month; for 30 days of brewing your own coffee, it would cost $7.50 while buying coffee at a cafe would cost $90. It's not rocket science; it's a ton of money to buy your coffee at a cafe. The only caveat would be if you were staying in the cafe to meet someone or work then it would make more sense, but if you are buying coffee to-go from a café, you're seriously messing up.

Groom Yourself

Self-care can add up fast for both men and women, especially when everyone is so concerned with their appearance. Since I was 18 years old, I have never paid for a haircut. How you ask? It's because I learned to cut my own hair and never looked back since! Don't worry, in actuality, I do check the back. Jokes.

When I was younger, I shaved my head which is the easiest way to cut your own hair. Now I use a combination of scissors, electric clippers, and a razor. People think I get my haircut at a salon. Everyone is always baffled when I tell them I cut it myself. Paying $50 for a haircut or paying $50 for one set of electric clippers that work worldwide once every 5 years, what do *you* think sounds more efficient? For an incredible amount of fun, let's consider the yearly cost comparison. Paying for a haircut monthly would add up to $600 a year, where cutting your own would be $10. I've shocked myself!

I got so good at it that when I was younger and still in

university, I cut my friend's hair, both men and women, in exchange for beer. That seemed like a fair trade to me! It made me feel good when my good friend Ben drove an hour to have me cut his hair.

Cheaper Dates (and friend activities)

Another area you can save big money with is when doing activities with your friends or going on dates. The idea of a traditional date usually involves an expensive meal and entertainment such as a movie or concert. In this outdated model, the man would always pick up the check as well. If you're following this classic model or even splitting the bill, this can add up incredibly fast.

When you first meet someone, there is no reason to go spending all your money on them – especially because it might not work out anyways. I'd feel stupid if I went and dropped $100 on a date with someone only to not hear from them again.

Going out to grab a coffee and sitting in a park, will cost just a few dollars instead of hundreds of dollars to wine and dine somebody. For fun, so much fun, let's assume we go on four traditional-style dates a month at $100 and split the bill – this would be $200 a month. If we changed those four dates a month to coffee dates, we'd spend $12 a month.

If the person thinks you're cheap for not spending big

money, and doesn't want to see you again, good riddance; that's a blessing because they just saved you from wasting your time on someone with backward priorities. If someone can't enjoy the little things in life, then they're not worth your time in the first place. This is why it's good to filter these types of people before meeting them in the first place.

Going on a simple date and splitting the bill, will attract the right types of people and you'll save money in the process. I've had so many lovely experiences going on simple dates in beautiful nature areas. The whole point is getting to know someone, so there's no need to spend a bunch of money when talking is free. In the end, this can save you thousands of dollars in the long run and have the benefit of filtering out superficial gold diggers.

It is hard to quantify some of the other savings strategies because everyone will save a different amount, but we can easily calculate the savings per year from just the monthly expenditure reduction ideas of exercising for free, make drinking cheaper, skipping the cafe, grooming yourself, and going on cheaper dates. If you were to go with all the more expensive options, you'd spend a whopping $10,500 on these items per year, if we go with my cheaper alternatives you'd spend just $964! I'm frugal automatically but seeing these comparisons is really eye-opening to how much money it's possible to save.

Save on Income Taxes

Let's discuss taxes while on the topic of savings. Nobody likes paying taxes, especially if the government mismanages the money it collects. Unfortunately, if you don't pay your taxes, you'll end up going to jail for tax evasion. The good thing is that there are lots of opportunities to save a lot of money with your taxes. The best way to go about maximizing your tax savings is by learning how to file your own taxes and to take advantage of the rules that benefit you.

If you decide to start your own business, especially one that includes a lot of expenses, you'll be able to offset your income by deducting all your business-related expenses. For example, since I am a travel writer, almost everything that I pay for while living around the world can qualify as an expense for my business. My major expenses including flights, accommodation costs, and food which all can be deducted from my income at the end of the year. The caveat is that the only way this is possible is because I have my own business. If you're working for someone then, unfortunately, there isn't much wiggle room on the amount of income taxes you are required to pay. It pays to be an entrepreneur!

Investment Strategies

So far, we've talked about how to save money, but now, let's talk about how we can make our money that we've saved work for us. This section will introduce several investment strategies that will help your money grow on its own.

Stock Trading

Near the time that I went away for my exchange study program in Bangkok, Thailand, was also the time that I started investing in the stock market. The real estate financial crisis had just ended in 2008, and the market began to rebound right when I got started. This meant that you could put your money into any company and it was almost guaranteed a huge return on investment.

Over the following three to four years, I made a 400% return on my stock investments. I often took my gains and reinvested them in other stock purchases along the way. The strategy that worked best came from buying and holding solid companies over the years. This went on for about five years in total, but then something changed. I became a bit anxious, and I wanted to make more money, the greed was growing inside of me. I built false confidence of trading over the years and thought that I could transfer the skills I thought I had learned into day trading to make money even faster.

Day-trading volatile stocks is incredibly riskier than holding solid and dependable companies long-term. Some would argue that it's gambling. The prices rise and fall so quickly; the object is to try and make money in both directions. Generally, day traders are leveraging money which amplifies the risks and the rewards. Trading on margin or leveraging is when the bank allows someone to borrow money to make trades, often at fairly substantial interest rates.

At the beginning of my day trading, I started out slowly, trading small amounts each time, but as time went on, I ramped up to larger trade sizes. I got to the point of trading $20,000 to $40,000 per trade and wasn't thinking much of it. Sadly, I soon found myself losing more money than I was making. I studied a lot, but I still couldn't seem to get ahead of the curve. Every once in a while, I'd make a big gain, such as the time I made $4,000 in 30 minutes. Even though I was losing overall, each gain made me think I was getting closer to winning.

I learned that, ultimately, stock trading really comes down to having control of your emotions. Even though I knew logically the right decision in many instances, often I would make the wrong decision and end up with another loss. Over a year, I racked up a nearly $20,000 loss. For a man in his mid-20s, this was enough to make me rethink what I was doing and eventually stop. I knew that at the rate I was going, I'd lose all of my money.

After a few months of sulking and being crushed by losing a considerable chunk of my savings, I ended up getting back in the game and eventually earned back a little bit of my money, reducing the loss to $14,000.

Looking back, I can see everything very clearly. I learned what it's like to be overcome with false confidence and greed. My mistake was that I got in a rush to make money and ignored logic, letting my emotions take over. Now, I can agree with all of the traditional stock investment advice of buying and holding conservative companies instead of looking for a quick gain. In the long run, it will definitely put you farther ahead. It's better to make a 5% to 10% return consistently over the years than to make 20% one year and then lose 40% the next. Don't get greedy!

I know that was a bit of a long introduction to stock trading, but it's important to learn early on that this is not a place to get rich quick. When trading, always think of the big picture and be conservative; you're better to keep what you have, then to lose it. From the beginning of the invention of the stock market to now, there's an obvious upward trend. The safest strategy is just to continue riding this trend.

The easiest strategy to ride the trend of the entire market is by buying index funds. These are funds that are made up of companies that represent the market as a whole; when the market is up, so are you, but when it's down, you are as well. For a novice, buying individual stocks can be quite time-consuming and difficult in the beginning, especially considering the type of market condition you buy at. Ultimately, you have to be willing to ride the wave for a long period of time, so don't invest money that you need access to soon.

Bank Investments

Banks generally offer a slew of investment options to grow your money in an even more conservative manner. Bank investments usually won't go over 5%, but that's better than nothing! These common bank investments include money market accounts, bonds, CDs, and savings accounts. All, on average, will yield a couple of percentage points per year. This is by far the safest route.

There are tons of ways to save money and make your money grow; it all starts with creating a plan. If you don't have a goal in mind, it's hard, if not impossible, to get where you want to go. This is why, from the start, we need to set up and determine our monthly spending requirements. I recommend keeping a savings of six months to a year worth of expenses in case something happens and you no longer have income.

It's important to develop good habits to erase the bad and be able to truly identify what you need versus what you simply want. This simple question is the driving force behind every aspect of my life. If any of your spending is out of whack, it's very easy to quickly self-sabotage. On the flipside, don't drive yourself crazy by being too frugal or cheap. Finding a happy medium where you're able to save money after your expenses is a great place to be. Overall, I recommend a combination of all the lessons I discussed for the greatest chance of success.

CHAPTER 5
MINIMALISM

Living a minimalist lifestyle has greatly improved my rate of saving and reduced the number of physical possessions that I had, ultimately leading me to a more stress-free existence. First, allow me to rant about modern-day excessive consumerism. Society is currently set up with many backward priorities, especially when it comes to buying. The United States is known for having the largest consumer economy in the world. Most Americans are constantly buying in order to have the latest consumer product and to keep up with the Joneses. There are many negative side effects from all of this buying, including lots of excess waste and stress.

The Problem with Mindless Consumerism

From all of my travels, I have learned that unnecessary buying is not restricted to the United States at all, actually as the world develops, consumerism is spreading all over like a virus. No matter where we go, everywhere we look we are bombarded with advertisements, constantly begging for our attention to try and convince us to buy more. Companies are pushing their agendas by imploring social media influencers, celebrities, and news media with huge followings to try and push us to buy. No matter who you are, you're told that if you don't have the latest item, you're unsuccessful. We're made to feel that we are always deficient when in reality, most of us have everything we actually need in life. Focusing on what we don't have is a perfect way to always be miserable.

A society that has its focus on mindless consuming means that society is more focused on temporary happiness from buying than lasting fulfillment from solving the root of the problem in our mindset in the first place. Material success is not a recipe for lasting happiness, as I'm sure most of you know.

The whole system is rigged!

Products are designed to become obsolete quickly forcing us to buy the newest version. Each purchase comes with an increased level of stress because we have to not only manage all of these items but maintain them as well. When we aren't using our precious time to take care of what we already bought, we use it for researching which item to buy next. It's difficult to identify that most of us are stuck on the hamster wheel of buying because so many people are also in the same boat.

Even though our purchases are mostly only valued by how much we've paid for them, in actuality, we are buying these items with our most valuable commodity, time. As our time alive is finite, are we really using our time in the wisest way?

For many of us, it's easy to get caught up in the cycle of senseless buying because it temporarily makes us feel content with what we have. After every purchase, we get a little high feeling, but it only last for a short time; once it fades, we have to buy the next item to get the high again. In that moment, we feel complete, although it's only temporary.

If we analyze it deeper, we can understand what's causing this feeling of needing more. By focusing on being appreciative for what we have, we can fix the problem indefinitely. The temporary fix of buying more is like putting a Band-Aid on a broken leg, which actually needed a cast. Shopping is merely a distraction from focusing on the root cause of the problem. It is possible to break free from endless, mindless consumerism with all of its negative impacts on our lives with a slight adjustment to how we see the world.

The solution comes from simply appreciating what we already have. All of my living abroad and traveling has taught me that people don't need many physical possessions to feel satisfied, healthy, and happy. There've been many times I've been traveling and witnessed people living in squalor, but they were immensely happy. Maybe they only had a few raggedy clothes on, but they all had huge smiles on their faces. They sure looked a lot happier than rich businessmen, driving their luxury cars filled with road rage, which seems to be a lot more common of a thing to see these days. The fascinating, yet sad part about this, is that society would consider the rich businessman a success and not the poor happy person. Our priorities are backward.

The Solution to Mindless Consumerism

The only difference between these two people is a difference in how they see the world. It doesn't matter how much material possessions you have; what matters is how thankful you are. This is choosing to be an optimist and recognizing that the glass is half full instead of half empty. Instead of focusing on all the things that we don't have, we need to change our focus to all of the things that we do have and truly appreciate them. In practical terms, this means being thankful for things that actually matter such as being alive, a habitable planet, our freedom, and family. It's a miracle that we have even come into existence.

As far as material possessions and money go, after a

level of comfortable living is achieved, earning more money or purchasing more items will not make us feel any more satisfied over the long term.

In addition to being appreciative, focusing on experiences instead of endless buying will also help to make us full complete. Once we have our priorities set correctly, realizing that we don't need to keep buying, we can focus on meaningful experiences such as moving abroad. These rewarding experiences will help us to develop our minds so that we can attain lasting fulfillment.

For me, overcoming constant challenges during my lifestyle living abroad has helped me come to this very real liberation. It is because of learning lessons like this that have made me such an advocate for encouraging others to step out of their comfort zones and overcome barriers. Remember that nothing outside of our bodies, in the physical world, shall provide us with lasting fulfillment. Instead, because we control our minds and the way we interpret the world, we are in complete control of our own fulfillment. Everything comes down to how we look at the world and the choice to appreciate what we have.

The Purge

Once our brains are thinking positively, minimalism will start to make a lot more sense. As I mentioned, minimalism is rooted in focusing on what we actually need, as opposed to what we simply want. Once we properly identify what we actually need and what we don't, we can rid ourselves of all of the things that aren't providing any real value to our lives. Go through all of the things you own and ask yourself if you really need the item or not. If you've had something for months and haven't used it, there is a good chance that you can probably get rid of it. By selling our unneeded items, we can build our savings, so we are serving two purposes. I was personally able to earn tons of money over the years by selling off all of my items I no longer needed.

Being able to identify needs and wants is the foundation of a minimalist lifestyle and also a way to save lots of money in day-to-day life by constantly considering if you actually need to purchase something or not.

When I first started living abroad, I had one large suitcase that would fit all of my life possessions that I would lug around from country to country. This one suitcase was around 50 lbs or 22.6 kgs. Over time, this only got heavier and heavier as I consumed more items. My professional photography career also required me to purchase more equipment, and this single suitcase suddenly turned into two large suitcases. This was still within the limits of most airline baggage policies, but it was starting to wear on my mind without me noticing.

I realized I was lugging around these large suitcases and

only using about half of the contents. It was taking lots of my energy to manage all of this stuff, which was subconsciously stressing me out and adding a burden to my life. I kept thinking that eventually, I would use this gear for a project, but the project never came.

I considered selling it, but kept putting it off and continued dragging the stuff around from country to country. Monetarily the value was only a few hundred dollars, but the unmeasurable mental strain was way more than I realized. One day, it all eventually clicked, and I realized that I simply didn't need this stuff anymore. I was able to sell a majority of the items and got some pocket money in the process. The mental weight and physical burden were suddenly lifted off of me, and it felt great!

Once I started downsizing, I couldn't stop. After coming to the realization that keeping only what I needed would better my life, I suddenly wanted to get rid of every unneeded thing that I had. I became very passionate about downsizing and eventually worked my way all the way down to one carry-on luggage and a small laptop bag.

Traveling around with such a small amount of items makes life so incredibly easy. I'm now constantly engulfed in a feeling of freedom knowing that I can pack up all of my material possessions in about 10 minutes and be on my way to wherever I want to go in the world.

My lifestyle doesn't lock me to any one place and now, neither do my possessions.

Also, around this point in my life, I had decided to pursue my travel blog full-time. From a practical standpoint, it made sense not to have to wait at baggage carousels for the rest of my life.

Adopting minimalism and having to take care of fewer possessions has a ton of benefits; some are quite obvious while some are more difficult to notice at first glance. Clearing unneeded distractions, whether their physical possessions or emotional baggage, will help you to focus your life on what's truly important. Once we can get rid of all of the distractions, we can prioritize purpose in our lives. When we have a purpose, we are happier and feel fulfilled.

You may still be confused about how to put a minimalist lifestyle into practice if you are newly introduced to the concept. Just to be clear, being a minimalist does not mean you have to wear rags, live in a mud hut, and only eat rice and drink water. All it means is getting rid of the excess and not buying more of it as life goes on. Excess possessions are distractions, weighing us down and burdening our minds. Even when something might seem like a simple purchase, that simple purchase could actually cause a great deal of stress.

Nothing is free; there is a cost to everything.

Our actual requirements in life are so simple, such as air, food, water, and shelter – anything beyond that you don't need to survive. Regardless, please don't forget to wear pants.

For myself, an example would be to keep clothing, even though I've had it for a while. I realize that having the latest fashion will not bring me lasting happiness. Eventually, my clothes do wear out, and I do have to buy new ones, but I'm able to save money by not having to take care of many clothes. I own a polo shirt that I bought ten years ago for $10; that's $1 a year to wear that shirt, and it still looks new!

Another technique we can utilize is to repurpose things that we already have. Recently, I was very proud of myself that I took a pair of pants that had gotten a little bit worn and instead of just throwing them away, I cut off the legs and sewed them into a pair of really comfortable shorts. They fit perfectly, and it was a really enjoyable process. Make the most of what you have and appreciate everything.

No matter what things we consume, whether too many possessions or too much food, too much alcohol, etc., excess of nearly everything will only bring negative impacts on our lives. The idea that having more is better is simply wrong. When you have excess, you will become a slave to your possessions. They will take control of your time and own you instead of you owning them.

I've been able to use the same point and shoot camera as well as the same iPhone for many years; I will use them until they break. If the item is getting the job done in a satisfactory way, then you don't need to replace it. Is it a need or a want? Living within our means is also better for the environment, as we produce less waste and pollution.

I just want to reiterate that focusing on experiences will bring the most reward. Instead of focusing on filling voids temporarily, focus on unique experiences like traveling, living abroad, treating your body well, self-development, and our loved ones. Instead of blowing money on superficial garbage like fashion trends, buy a plane ticket. Go invest your time in learning that language you always wanted to learn. Overcoming challenges will bring far more real value.

In conclusion, many modern societies have embraced a set of backward priorities. We have been pushed into buying material possessions which don't make us feel complete in the long run. Once the high of our new purchase wears off, we feel like we need to buy more to get back to that feeling of completeness. In actuality, the solution to feeling like we always need more can be found through appreciating what we have and not what we don't. Once our priorities are straight, all the wanting of unneeded items will drift away. The urges will be gone. We can then focus on experiences that give us real personal development through overcoming challenges.

CHAPTER 6
PASSIVE INCOME

What makes my lifestyle of living abroad truly
sustainable is because of a little piece of magic called
passive income. Over the years, I've had a ton of
traditional businesses that require active attention and
also several passive income streams that only require
major effort in the beginning. The beauty of a passive
income stream is that once it's up and running, it
requires very minimal effort to continue reaping the
rewards. For most people, I believe that a combination
of both active and passive income is best. Ideally, if we
can build up enough passive income streams to
completely cover our basic living expenses, then we can
use our precious time to focus on other meaningful parts
of life. This could mean focusing on experiences
mentioned before or focusing on projects that may not
generate lots of money but do give a lot of purpose to

our existence. Having these basic cost-of-living expenses taken care of can put our minds at ease, greatly reducing stress.

In the beginning, the idea of passive income might feel completely unattainable, or perhaps, like a fairytale. It can almost seem too good to be true that we could have businesses that pay regularly and consistently and that don't require a bunch of continuous effort. The thing about it is it's not that crazy if we break it down into a step-by-step process like everything else.

The passive income streams don't have to be a lot individually as long as they add up to your requirements. This chapter is all about getting our brains working so we can develop our own passive income streams. What you come up with might not be the ones that I specifically recommend, but it doesn't have to be. We all must utilize our own strengths in creating businesses that will be suitable for us.

The passive income streams that I have generated throughout my life have now paid for my living expenses for the past five years. Another comforting thing to consider is that there are literally unlimited passive income opportunities we just have to be creative in our thinking to create them.

When I was just getting started in business, I focused mostly on businesses that simply generated money. I was less concerned about giving my life purpose and more about stacking up dough. Dollar, dollar bill y'all! Some of my businesses were my hobbies, but others were simply just to make money like re-selling used electronics online. I believe that this is acceptable in the beginning when we are working to gain experience to figure out what direction we would like to take. However, once we become a little bit more financially secure, we must make a conscious decision to choose businesses that benefit the greater good. This will make our lives more rewarding by giving ourselves purpose and simultaneously helping others. It's important that we focus on activities in life that agree with our morals.

Don't put all of your eggs in one basket.

Just as with common investment advice, I'd strongly recommend working to create several passive income streams so you won't be significantly affected if one fails. It's all about creating an insurance policy for your income. I'm not suggesting to not pay full attention to one project while creating the passive income stream; I'm simply saying that after you create one successful passive income, keep creating more until you feel secure.

My passive income streams are now made up of book publishing royalties, rental income, advertisement income, and affiliate marketing income. This ensures that even if one disappeared, I would have something else to fall back on. Don't worry; I will discuss all of these passive incomes and more below.

Without further ado, I give to you my most viable passive income streams while living a life abroad.

Dividend Stocks

As you know from earlier, I created my first business of hustling candy on the streets when I was nine years old. Over the years since then, I've created and operated several active income businesses. It wasn't until age 20 when I finally generated my first passive income. This very first passive income stream was with dividend stocks, which are a type of stock that have scheduled payouts, sort of like a bonus for owning the stock. When I first started investing in normal stocks, I learned about dividend stocks as well. At the time, it really didn't matter where I put my money because as of the 2008 market rebound, I made money with practically every single stock I purchased. It's a great feeling to be going along and see that additional money is being deposited into your account, without having to do any additional work. Basically, dividend stocks are like a machine that prints money!

However, just like with normal stocks, dividend stocks can also fluctuate in their price. Therefore, even if a dividend stock is paying a good return through dividends, if the value of the stock is decreasing, you might not be making any money, or you might even lose money in the process. This is why I would recommend staying away from dividend stocks that pay too high of dividends because they tend to be very volatile. As they say, if it looks too good to be true, it probably is. More conservative and solid companies offer less dividend yield but are more consistent and bring less risk in the process. There's really no point to invest in a dividend stock which pays 20% in dividends but is going to drop 50% in value.

All of the major brokerages out there offer some sort of web interface and stock screener tool which you can use to easily find dividend stocks to buy. Also, a simple Google search will help you narrow down dividend stocks that you may be interested in. If it's your first time investing in stocks, it is also important to consider the brokerage fees involved in buying and selling. Some brokerages charge a whole lot more for trading than others, so be aware of this before choosing. Other brokerage fees to look out for are inactivity fees which can add up quickly if you take a break and forget about your account like I did.

In the end, if you choose more conservative companies, you can expect to make between 4% to 8% annually on dividend yields, which is a very nice supplement to your income.

Review Website with Affiliate Links

When I moved back to Thailand for the second time, I moved into a shared housing environment. The house was filled with all types of people including local Thai people as well as foreigners who had a variety of jobs and businesses. It was a diverse crowd and included people with all types of occupations including a dive instructor, graphic designer, magazine editor, business consultant, Internet marketer, and a pair of English teachers.

It seemed like there was something to learn from everyone there with all their unique backgrounds and life experiences. There were a lot of interesting viewpoints to consider with people coming from everywhere around the world. During that time, I really bonded with people, and it became like a family even though there was the occasional drama. The house was situated at the end of a dead-end, quiet Bangkok street. It was super peaceful and had lots of tropical vegetation, fruit, an outdoor pool, comfortable living space, and a big kitchen; it was truly an oasis.

There was one online marketer that lived there who I became close friends with; his name was Wilding. Wilding was the man who initially gave me the idea to create a website with product reviews. The review website business model was fairly simple. The website had a host of product reviews, and if a reader were interested in buying a product, they'd click an affiliate link. This link would take them to Amazon, and if they ended up purchasing anything, the business would receive an affiliate commission in the process. You've heard of Amazon, right?

Each time someone would successfully purchase a product it would generate around a 5% profit. I was very intrigued by this because the only initial setup costs were to buy the domain name, acquire the website hosting which I already had, and produce the content. I ended up paying someone to write for me; in this case, I hired Wilding's father who wrote several reviews about camera tripods. The beauty is that the type of product you write about can be something that you are actually interested in. Choose something you're passionate about, and it won't feel like work.

Outsourcing the article writing, was a concept that I had initially learned from *The 4-Hour Workweek* written by Tim Ferriss. This book had a very strong impact on my life and truly shaped my future. It changed the way I looked at the world, especially in business and voila, here I am today.

Once the website was running like an oiled machine, I stopped working on it and moved to other projects. I could've spent time marketing the website to drive traffic, but I was an amateur and dropped the ball. Over the next couple of years, the website paid off a few times over, and I made a decent gain of about 100% profit. It was a major success in considering the percentage return on investment, but I didn't fully take advantage of this because I didn't drive more traffic to increase profits. Perhaps it was because it was something I just wasn't super passionate about. Regardless, it was a fun little experiment to see what was possible with affiliate links. Nowadays, I still use affiliate links in my blog, which I'll discuss later in this chapter, so keep reading!

Income from Subletting

After living in the wonderful shared house for a while in Bangkok, there ended up being some privacy concerns, some drama, and at that point, I just wanted my own space. After an episode of drama, I began my search for a place of my own. Not far from the shared house I found a conveniently located condominium with lots of incredible features.

The condo I found was in an area that I already knew and loved, was near public transportation, had a nice pool, gym, and sauna, as well as friendly staff. I moved to this condo for the following couple of years and became friends with the manager of the building. When I first started renting, I was on the ground floor in a very comfortable unit that looked out to a small jungle. Even though I was in the middle of the city, I got to live in another peaceful little oasis!

After renting for a little while, I learned there was another unit available on the top floor with a much different city view. Long story short, the other condo was better in some ways, worse in others but ultimately I gave it a shot. During this process of condo hunting, I realized that it was quite hard to locate reasonable accommodations as a foreigner in Bangkok for a shorter period of time without spending tons of money in the process. This is why, instead of letting go of my first condo, I decided to list it on Airbnb and see if I could rent it while living in the other unit.

Within a very short time of posting, I was contacted by a French woman who wanted to rent for three months. I was thrilled! Actually, I listed the condo for double the price I was paying for it, which was still an incredible deal for a traveler. A real win-win if I say so myself. This generated enough profit to pay for my new rent, so I basically got to live rent-free for the following three months. It was the perfect scenario.

This turned out to be a great option for me, but there are some factors to consider before you do this yourself. Many times, landlords are not interested in having you sublet their place, and it might even be against their rules. Be careful. I actually didn't check with the owner of the condo to see if it was possible. I was young, dumb, and decided to just go for it. It all worked out for me, and nobody was the wiser. I wouldn't recommend breaking the rules because you might get thrown out of the building and lose your income. It can work however if you figure out a way to do it and not make anybody angry. Be creative.

The whole part about being able to pay your living expenses with a passive income will take a massive burden off your shoulders. For that entire three months, I remember feeling like I was walking on a cloud everywhere I went. Living rent-free is the best!

Publish a Book

During the time of living in Bangkok, I studied Thai language at a local private Thai language school. It was at that school where I met a very talented book author. Actually, the author was the principal of the school and very a talented teacher as well. I learned a lot from him in the classroom each day, and one day, I learned that he was actually putting the final touches on his book, *How to Read Thai in 10 Days* by Bingo Lingo. He was incredibly swamped with all of his workload he had from the school and didn't really have time to focus on getting a book published. This is where I saw an opportunity and one day asked if he would take a meeting with me.

We met over coffee, and I pitched him my idea to publish his book, create a website to sell it, and in exchange receive a portion of the proceeds. I didn't ask for any money up front and offered my online marketing in addition to drive sales. I can't remember now if I mentioned it in the first meeting with him, but I had actually never published a book in my life. Plot twist!

Luckily like many other skills, I was able to research the topic online and learned all of the intricacies of the book publishing process. Over time, I learned more and more and now feel very confident when it comes to publishing a book on Amazon.

About four years later and our initial agreement and partnership is still going strong. We are both reaping the rewards of publishing and collected payment for an average of 100 book sales a month. Generally, it's enough to pay a majority of my rent in most countries that I choose to live in. This income has been a huge lifesaver for both myself and the author who has now quit his job at the school.

Before having the book royalty income, my businesses weren't always the most consistent because I'd work from project to project. The beauty of book publishing and becoming an author is that it takes very little to get started. Literally, anybody can write their own book. I've seen all sorts of garbage for sale on Amazon which may be comforting or may be sad.

I must admit that the process of writing a full-on book is actually incredibly intimidating. However, just like with everything else, if you break it down into steps, or in this case chapters, it becomes just a series of smaller writings. If you're a blogger, you can think about it as a series of longer blog posts. The hardest part, as always, was just getting started, but once I made a game plan, created a timeline for myself, the project began picking up steam, and I breezed through the whole book writing process.

I can't wait to publish this book! I'm thrilled because I primarily wanted to create a helpful resource for those of you who are interested in how to live abroad. The bonus is that I'll create another passive income stream for myself. I know what you're thinking, but no, I didn't write this book for only the income. The income that will generate is merely a bonus.

I plan to write more and more, both books and articles, focused on topics that bring people together and inspire everyone to pursue their dreams, in order to move the world in a positive direction. I am certain that everyone reading this has a topic that they too are passionate about and could easily write a book about. You can take literally any interest that you have, break it down into chapters, create an outline, and write a book to publish yourself. Consider how you can bring value to people's lives and hopefully how you can make the world a better place.

Don't be shy; get out there champ and write a book! You might get a bonus of developing a passive income stream in the process.

Passive Blog Income

My beautiful baby blog was first conceived in the year 2014. In the beginning, my blog strictly came about because I was obsessed with food and still am to this day; a true passion that has never faded. Actually, the initial idea came from an English friend of mine while we were eating at a Vietnamese restaurant in Thailand. I was taking photos, as I normally did before it was such a popular activity, and she suddenly suggested that I become a food blogger.

It's funny, until that day, I had never thought about it before, but when she said it, the idea completely clicked in my head, and I was hooked. Within 24 hours of that conversation, I bought the domain name and created the website, PierreAteIt.com. As you can imagine, I blogged strictly about food, focusing mostly on cheap and tasty food around Bangkok.

On a side-note, my friend Kate, who first inspired me to start my blog, suddenly disappeared from my life not too long after that. I think she ran off and married an Australian. I haven't been able to track her down since, so Kate, if you read this, get in touch with me; you sent my life on a wild ride!

As time went on, I realized that I didn't want to be restricted to only food and expanded my focus into travel and lifestyle as well as switching over my former business domain name to PIERREBLAKE.com. After a few years of blogging, I finally started seeing some decent traffic coming in. It was at that point I decided to finally place some advertisements on my website.

Website Advertisements

First and foremost, I am not a big fan of advertisements at all, as you can probably figure out from my rants. Especially because I have no control over what content they are placing all over my website. Luckily, Google tends to promote businesses related to mine, but it's still not my favorite thing in the world. However, it's hard to pass up the passive income stream when the advertisements don't really change the user experience of the website. I started with more advertisement units per page, but have recently downsized to two ad units per page in hopes to make the ads even less obtrusive. You're welcome, my loyal readers!

These website advertisements provide a little money every month to help pay my bills. I know some blogger friends who make tons of money a month via their advertisements. I'm not becoming wealthy off of them, but at least I can see what's possible in the future.

My only recommendation would be that if you go the advertisement route, be conservative and don't let them interfere with the quality of your content. If you're just starting out with your blog, chances are you won't even have enough traffic to make it worthwhile anyway. Don't bombard your users with advertisements especially if they aren't even generating much money. Use them with caution and advertisements can be a decent way to build yet another passive income stream.

Blog Affiliate Links

Another passive income stream that is generated through my website comes from affiliate links. As I mentioned before, the affiliate links in my previous review website generated money every time someone bought a product on Amazon that originated from my website. Take that concept and transform it slightly and you'll get my current business model.

For my travel blog, I write a lot of hotel review articles; within them are links to hotel booking websites where readers can make reservations. As you probably pieced together, if the affiliate link originates on my website, I will receive a small commission for each sale.

This provides a very modest income stream, but it's something substantial enough and definitely adds to my lifestyle. I only promote the affiliate links that I feel good about. I'm not keen to promote a bunch of garbage just to make money. I would never sell my soul! I focus mainly on hotel bookings but occasionally branch out into other related products and services depending on what I'm writing about.

As long as you don't sacrifice your morality, then affiliate links can be a great way to generate a passive income stream.

These are the main ways that my blog generates money. Advertisements and affiliate links generate a modest income that helps pay for my living expenses. I also make much more money from sponsored articles and social media posts, but those are on a project basis, so I'll discuss those more in detail in the active income chapter.

Rental Property

I was exposed initially to real estate investments when I was rather young because my father owned rental property for most of my childhood. When I was younger, he started with a four-unit apartment building. As I got older, I watched him expand from four-units to ten-units. I recognized early that real estate could be a great way to build a passive income stream, but I didn't imagine that I could actually do it for myself for a long time because I thought I needed more income. For a very long time, I wrote off the idea as something that I wouldn't be able to do until I saved up more money to pay cash or had a steady income to qualify for a mortgage. With my sporadic income, it just didn't seem possible to buy a home for a while. Luckily, I learned many years later that I was completely wrong in my thinking and could have afforded a house when I first graduated university at age 22 if I just paid cash. It would have been nice to know this back then, but things seemed to all work out for me.

For six years after graduating from university, I spent most of my time focusing on active income streams for a majority of my income. I had the book royalty coming in for a while but still had to actively work on other businesses to survive. I was able to save money that entire time as well and kept my eyes open for more passive income opportunities that would appear.

At that time, I could live comfortably knowing that my bills were paid and didn't have any real financial limitations. Just a couple years back, I was catching up with a close friend named Georgia who I had previously lived with at a shared house while in University. I learned that she had bought multiple rental properties in the Midwest of the United States and it got my brain wheels turning. She had a regular job, so she was able to qualify for mortgages. I knew I still wouldn't qualify for a mortgage, but I decided to look for real estate online anyways. I came to find out that there were rental properties available for sale for far less than I ever would have imagined. I struck gold! These were so cheap that they didn't require a mortgage at all; I could simply pay for them with the cash from my savings. It was easy because my money was already liquid, sitting in the bank, patiently waiting for my next investment after my fiasco with stock trading.

I think one of the reasons I wasn't able to realize this was possible was because I grew up in an area where housing prices were so much more expensive than what I was finding. In my hometown, it would have been the deal of a century to find a house for $100,000. Now, I was learning that you could buy houses for less than $50,000. These weren't houses that needed a bunch of work to rent but did require some.

I did some more research and within a few months found and visited several rental properties in a convenient area between my family members. Some needed a lot of work that I just wasn't prepared for. Once I found one I liked, I moved quickly and bought it. My friends and family didn't approve initially and thought I was crazy for buying such cheap houses.

It did turn out that this house did require a bit of work, but in the long run, it all paid off. The quality construction of a house that was nearly 80 years old was impressive; it was built like a tank. I still own the property to the day of writing this book and plan to hold onto it for years to come.

My multiple rental properties generate between 15% and 30% net profit yearly, averaging in the low 20s. This is basically unheard of when it comes to real estate. Through trial and error, I was able to put together a strategy that has worked fantastically for me and can work for you as well!

Research

Location is incredibly important for all businesses, including investment properties. The first city I tried had lots of options that were in my price range, but they were just too far of a drive. Luckily, I found an alternative city that was more conveniently located.

Take the time to learn about the area; know where you should buy and where you shouldn't. It's important that your tenants have a safe place to live, which I need to remind you is your responsibility as a landlord.

The second part of the research, apart from location, comes down to price. I often use Zillow.com for my research, but there are other tools available as well. With Zillow, you can find previous sale prices of houses in the neighborhood to figure out if you're getting a deal or not. This way you'll be able to make sure you'll profit in the future when you decide to sell.

Property Inspection & Future Repair Cost Estimation

Now that you know how much a comparable home can sell for in your area, you'll need to start viewing homes to estimate how much work the investment property will require. Before buying my first house, I didn't know anything about how much repairs would cost. Luckily, through reaching out to people around me, I was able to establish a pretty decent idea of what each major repair would run.

Repair costs change greatly based on location, so ask around in your prospective area. Feel free to call professionals for free quotes. Knowing your repair costs will allow you to estimate if you'll be able to make money or not.

Costly Repairs

> Roof
> Foundation
> Plumbing
> Heating and cooling (furnace/air conditioning)
> Windows
> Siding
> Electrical

Minor Repairs

> Paint
> Flooring
> Cosmetic issues

I recommend over-estimating all of your expenses, that way you'll account for unexpected costs that I guarantee are sure to arise. Also, remember to look for evidence of termites, mold, toxic contamination, etc., which have the potential to destroy a house's value or simply be too big of a hassle to deal with. Be sure to hire a trusted home inspector before making your final decision. I wasted my time with an inspector who was very biased before finding one who was more level-headed. Skipping hiring an inspector really bit me on my most recent purchase, so I can't stress enough how important this step can be!

When buying my first house, I looked at around 20 homes before I made my final decision. Don't get emotionally attached to any property or rush into a purchase as things can change fast. I would also recommend seeing several homes in one day, so you don't waste time driving to and from. Be sure to take excellent photos and detailed notes of each property including what repairs are required, so you don't confuse them later as I did.

Once you have inspected all the properties on your list and decided what repairs are needed, you'll be able to combine this with your other data to decide whether you can profit from purchasing or not.

Expect the Unexpected

I never would've imagined how many fees stack up after purchasing a house. When you hear someone is making a certain amount of rent per month, without prior knowledge, it's easy to be overly-optimistic on profit forecasts. For example, if someone tells you they charge $1,000 per month for their rental property, it's easy to overlook that they might be spending half of that or more on expenses.

Major Expenses

> - Closing costs
> - Government fees
> - Utilities
> - Insurance
> - Property taxes
> - Mortgage

Remember to budget in a cushion for other potential expenses that may arise. I'm really glad I did this because, within a week of buying my house, I ended up spending a few thousand dollars because the furnace broke which led to the house freezing and having to completely change out the plumbing system.

I was also happy I listened to my father who told me not to overextend myself financially. Always leave a decent amount of money in the bank so you still have money to live on and don't feel too stressed. No need to add extra stress to your life because you've spread yourself too thin!

Proper Negotiation

Even though you may be excited about a house, don't get emotionally attached, no matter how perfect it seems.

Remember that the one who cares least in negotiation has the most leverage. Remind yourself that this is an investment, spending too much on the purchase price decimates profit margins.

It's always better to offer a low price and then negotiate back up to a middle ground. This was the technique I used to get my first house for 32% off the sale price! If an owner won't move on the price, and it's too expensive, just move on and save yourself the hassle.

Property Management

This has less to do with how to purchase a rental property and more on how to save money and time with tenants. For me, it's pretty much impossible to manage a rental property from abroad. For this reason, I decided to hire a property management company. Management companies take the hassle out of a lot of the process, most of the time. This isn't always the case, but they're still worth having while living abroad.

The first big hassle would be doing a proper background check on a tenant applicant. My management company informed me of their screening process, and I was amazed at how thorough they are. Getting a deadbeat renter can absolutely destroy yearly profits. It doesn't matter if they paid all of their rent; if they destroy something or you have to evict them, say goodbye to that year of profit. Remember to make sure you get as big of a deposit as possible.

Major Benefits of Property Managers

- ➤ Tenant screening
- ➤ Creates a barrier between the landlord and tenant, so the landlord can't be taken advantage of as easily
- ➤ The tenant cannot contact the landlord directly and annoy them
- ➤ Management companies are often harder on the tenants than an individual, which leaves you less chance to lose money

After you've purchased your property, be sure to remember to immediately have the utilities changed over to the tenant's name. Also, have your tenants sign an affidavit which states that they will be responsible for utilities no matter the circumstances. Whether you are managing the property yourself or hire a property management company, be sure to understand the lease terms completely. If you don't like part of the contract, change it.

Rental properties can be incredibly passive or active depending on your personal preference. If you're willing to spend your time working on them, you can easily save money on labor but remember that you will also sacrifice your time that you could be working on other projects.

I now see the trajectory with real estate, and I look forward to growing my empire well into the future to create wealth for myself and my family for generations to come.

YouTube Channel

From a very young age, I'm talking about when I was in the single digits, I was very passionate about producing my videos. I started with my family's VHS camcorder to shoot all kinds of stuff. That camera didn't work very well, so in a few years time, I got my own camcorder when I was 11 or 12 years old. From then on, I wanted to be a professional film producer. Later in life, I ended up pursuing this as my business for about ten years of my life.

It all started when I moved away to university after graduating from high school. Video production provided an active income, which took a lot of time and effort. For most of my video career, I was working from project to project and will discuss more about this active income in the following chapter. It wasn't until early in 2010 when I first created a YouTube channel. A few years later, I was able to turn on advertisements that eventually generated a passive income from videos I had produced.

I had built up a few thousand subscribers that were viewing mostly music videos that I had created. Eventually, YouTube began advertisements on their website and allowed creators such as myself to turn on advertisements in their videos. Once again I'm not a huge fan of advertisements, but most of the time they're ignored anyway. I was sure not to turn on the super annoying ones. Every time someone viewed or clicked the ads, I might receive a small amount of money. This provided one more passive income stream to help assist with my bills. Nowadays, I have, for the most part, turned off my advertisements because my money comes from other streams.

There are tons of opportunities out there to pursue a life of making videos full-time. This sounds like a fantastic lifestyle to me! However, if you are able to generate a full-time income off of YouTube alone, then you will have to focus all of your time on creating the content. If you are working full-time on videos, then it won't be a passive income anymore, but an active one.

If you're passionate enough about creating videos and do want to devote all of your time to making them, then it is possible to make this a full-time job.

Create an Online Course

If you're very passionate about a hobby or possess some special skill, you can teach people by creating an online course. Just like with the book, by creating an online course, you can help a lot of people and also provide a passive income stream for yourself. If you're even remotely interested in creating an online course, I would recommend to just try.

It's best if you truly know what you're talking about to really give value to your students. That being said, any topic can be researched, and you can put together a compelling online course even if when you started you didn't know absolutely all of the ins and outs.

There are many websites out there that will host your online course and will only take a portion of the proceeds when your course actually sells. If you host the course yourself, you will have a lot less visibility online and may come up against other challenges such as people being able to simply steal it without paying. If not correctly configured, someone can just save your course and distribute it later for free.

A few years back, I created a how to become a blogger course that is still available on PIERREBLAKE.com at the time of writing this book. The process was very straightforward and has a lot in common with writing a book. I broke down the content into chapters and created a PowerPoint presentation for each chapter. Next, I took video of myself teaching and then edited it all together into a single video file. Finally, I posted it for sale on my own website and hosted the actual files on an Amazon server. That way, it was harder for people to steal the course. If you have a hobby or skill that you are an expert in, creating an online course can be a great way to generate a passive income stream.

Drop Shipping Store

I used to do Internet reselling online, and some of my suppliers were open to the idea of drop shipping. I will discuss in more detail later about my active income from buying products from China and then selling them on eBay. That business model included me shipping the products to myself, and then redistributing them to my customers.

However, with a drop shipping store, you can reduce this step and hassle by simply having your supplier ship your items directly to your customers. It's a similar concept to promoting affiliate links on your website. This is because you are basically being paid for linking together the buyers and sellers.

The more middle men you remove from the equation, the more profit you can make. When a new order comes in, you simply send it off to your supplier, and they will ship the order out on your behalf. The only problem that would arise is if your customer were unhappy, and then you are dealing with them instead of the product's manufacturer. However, if the product is fairly hasslefree, this could be a very good passive income opportunity. Once you set up a website that is churning out sales, it's basically set it, then forget it, and you've got a whole new passive income stream.

Stock Photo and Stock Video

If you are very talented with creating quality photos, videos, or both, you may have a chance at selling your content on stock video or stock photo websites. Not everyone can pass this test, but if you were a professional photographer or videographer at any point in your life, there's a large chance that you can.

Generally, the types of content that sell on stocks websites is more commercial oriented, so you'll have to shoot your content considering this theme. You have to figure out which stock photo or stock video services are best for you, and then you will have to submit an application to be considered for selling your content on their website. Once you pass the test you're able to submit your content, once your content is live then you simply sit back and collect your payments.

Once you have a large enough library, even if you're making a small amount for each piece of content, it all adds up and could be quite substantial in the end. A huge plus is that you basically don't have to do any additional work once your content is live.

When you really think about it, this is just the tip of the iceberg when it comes to passive income streams. In this chapter, I focused mainly on the passive income streams that I have generated, only stock video and drop-shipping are businesses that I have not done personally.

All in all, these will take some time to set up and will require some substantial work, but once you get them going the potential for large returns is very possible. Being paid automatically, no matter how much money you're making is a really great feeling. I've had some of these passive incomes for so long that I have begun to take them for granted, but writing this reminds me how great they are!

You don't have to limit yourselves to only what I have recommended; you can create tons of passive income streams by doing your own brainstorming and research. Passive income can be a great supplement to your active income and hopefully covers the cost of living while you're living abroad. There's no upside limit for potential earnings. I recommend that you build both passive and active income streams so that if one fails, you have the other as an insurance policy for the other.

CHAPTER 7
ACTIVE INCOME

As you now know, because you're so smart, it's important to balance both passive income and active income. Active income is the type of income that you have to work for actively. It's nice to have a passive income to cover the cost of living and pair it with an active income to give you some purpose in your life.

For me, this means having enough passive income to fund my lifestyle, that way I can focus my time on projects that I'm passionate about such as writing a book or writing my blog which makes less than some of my other incomes. Passive income offers some leniency to not feel so much pressure when deciding what we would like to pursue with the bulk of our time. In that way, passive income acts as an insurance policy for living expenses. If for some reason we cannot figure out our direction, we will have relief knowing that our cost of living is taken care of by passive income.

If you're only making an income for the sake of making money, you will never feel fulfilled in life. An active income should include projects that make you feel like you are doing something good for the world while also paying you for your time. At the end of the day, we need something to give us purpose to wake up for every morning.

When it comes to active income and living abroad, the types of business opportunities will vary from country to country. Some of the opportunities available in your home country will simply not be available in your new home. It's important to choose an active income that both excites you and offers the flexibility and freedom to live a lifestyle that you desire. In the end, we will be able to get a lot more accomplished while living abroad if we have the freedom to do as we please with our time. If our business requires long hours, then we'll have no free time to experience the new country or make any large strides in personal development.

Throughout the decade that I have spent living outside the United States, I have tried tons of different active income opportunities. There was a wide range that included acting in television commercials to running my online marketing business that had a handful of clients each paying me a monthly service fee. No matter which country I've lived in, I've been able to make it work financially, it's never impossible.

In the beginning, I was willing to try anything under the sun to earn an income and discovered what truly excited me in the process. When you're motivated to work and passionate about your business, there is also a good chance that you'll be able to grow a lot from your business. This chapter focuses on starting points to start earning active incomes including both jobs and entrepreneurial ventures. As with the chapter on passive income, these can be starting points in your brainstorming process if there's not something you find interest in. Most of what I have done has been in the creative field, and I understand that may not suit everyone.

Blogger

The active income that has given me the most freedom and unique opportunities in my life has been professional blogging. The beauty is that you can blog about absolutely anything you'd like! If there is a topic that excites you, then there is a good chance other people are also excited about the topic and voila, you have an opportunity to blog.

You'll have complete control over what you share, your work schedule, and also where you work from, which is key when living abroad. In the last chapter, I discussed how my blog makes passive income, including advertisements and affiliate links. However, I make a majority of my blog income through active income opportunities such as sponsored posts. These sponsored posts come in two forms; one type is sponsored blog posts and the other sponsored social media posts. I only accept opportunities that I feel completely comfortable accepting and that fit with my sense of morality.

I've been paid tens of thousands of dollars to promote products and services that my readers have genuine interest in. I would never sell my soul to promote a product or service that I don't believe in, don't worry! The majority of my sponsored social media post income comes from posting on Instagram.

As a travel blogger, I get to try things that normal tourists don't typically have access to, and I'm treated as a VIP guest in the process. You don't have to focus on being a travel blogger if your interest lies somewhere else. When you have a blog, there are unlimited opportunities to make money focused on a topic that excites you personally.

If you're interested in pursuing all types of blogging full-time, I've actually created an in-depth blog course which can be found on PIERREBLAKE.com.

Web Developer

I started creating websites when I was 11 years old, and have never stopped. When I became an adult, I decided to turn web design and development into a business. Over the years I've created hundreds of websites, some professional and some for my own interests. Being a web developer can also give you an immense amount of freedom. As a web developer, you'll have the freedom to work when and where you want as well as charging as much as you want.

Websites have become such an integral part of life that there will always be a demand for people who can create them. When it comes to website design and development, everything you need to know can easily be found online. This means that there is almost no barrier to entry; the only requirement is your time to learn, assuming you don't know already.

As far as getting new clients, when it comes to web design, I've found that it mostly comes down to your networking skills. People will generally hire web developers based on personal recommendations or from physically meeting you. More often than not, people tend to choose a web developer based on what their friends say.

Budgets for websites can range in a wide variety from a few hundred dollars all the way up to tens of thousands of dollars which ultimately gives you unlimited earning potential. Creating one website while living in a cheaper country might provide enough money to live on for a year.

Photographer

I was a professional photographer for about ten years of my life. Photography can offer an immense amount of freedom. If you want to be successful, you must have talent but also know how to offer great customer service. There is a reason that there are so many starving artists. Generally, artists lack social skills required to be a successful business person. However, if you have both social skills and a talent for photography you can be incredibly successful.

It is possible to learn how to take better photos, but I feel that people that are best at photography already see the world in an artistic way in the first place. As a photographer, a lot of your work will come down to being able to network.

While you are living abroad and getting started as a photographer, it might be easier to network and work with other foreigners as they generally will feel more comfortable working with you. To be clear, I'm simply referring to networking for business in this case. As far as living in a foreign country, networking for social reasons should be with local people.

While living in Thailand, I had clients from both foreign

backgrounds and local backgrounds. In the beginning, I did have more Western clientele.

As a disclaimer, when you turn your hobby into a business, it can ruin it. Suddenly, when something becomes work, it can become much less enjoyable to do in your free time. This is sad but true.

Internet Reseller

Another business that I have a great deal of experience with is Internet reselling. Internet reselling is basically the concept of finding a good price on a product and then selling it for profit online. It's not always easy to find a deal but when you do it should be easy to make a profit.

When I was younger, I focused on used electronics. I've bought and sold hundreds of products over the years always making a nice profit in the process. Searching hard and long for deals can be difficult and I have been burned a few times over the years where people do not deliver on what they were selling.

When I was 16, I bought shoes and apparel that was made in China and then resold it on eBay. Let's just say I was able to buy my first two cars with cash. I basically bought and sold whatever I could find! When I moved to university, I kept this going and focused on electronics such as laptops and cell phones. There were always students looking to sell their things to make quick money for who knows what! One time I bought a shoebox of new cell phones, I didn't ask how the person got them. With each resell I would focus on making at least 50% profit. If you see an opportunity, go for it, it's one of the easiest ways to earn cash.

English Teaching

I have not seen tons of English teachers making the most of their living abroad experience but sure with some effort and the right job it could be done. First and foremost, I have never been a full-time or part-time English teacher. I have dabbled in being an English tutor from time to time to make some side money which I could also recommend. Plus you get paid in cash so no need to worry about taxes! My route was to go for the upper-end clientele because I had business school education so I could therefore market myself as a "business English tutor" able to charge a premium price in the process.

While living in Hong Kong, I met a few English teachers that were able to make really good money and had a great quality of life, but sadly those stories are few and far between. This really comes down to the individual job. There are diamonds in the rough English teaching opportunities that would give more benefits.

It's important to note that there are also possibilities to

become an online English teacher working from anywhere, which would give way more freedom than a location dependent position. Food for thought!

Physical Trainer

While living in Thailand, I did all of the odd jobs out there to survive. I really hustled in these streets. Some of the people I've met along the way were physical trainers. In a lot of Asian countries, specifically there was a novelty for having a foreign physical trainer. This novelty could apply to several types of jobs. This is not always the case, but in some respects, you will be able to make more money than a local personal trainer.

Much like the other entrepreneurial ventures, you will have complete freedom of your time as you can schedule your clients whenever you wish, freedom to charge whatever rates you wish and freedom to choose where you'd like to do the training. As people become more and more interested in physical fitness, I can see this being a very lucrative career, especially being able to market yourself on social media, gaining a following to help grow your business. This is also a job in which you can be paid in cash.

Freelance Actor or Model

To be honest, I never really thought of myself as a professional actor or model, but when I moved to Asia, everything changed. Suddenly I was thrown into an environment where simply because of the way I looked, I was able to act in television commercials. When I first arrived in Bangkok, there was a strong demand for foreigners to participate in television commercials.

While in Thailand, I was hired for about 15 television commercials over a 2 year period. This made a good source of income which didn't require a ton of work. Lots of international brands produce their commercials in Southeast Asia to save money on production costs. Even if you don't necessarily fit the general requirements to be a model, I would still encourage you to give it a shot because many times they have several roles to fill.

As an extra, you basically get paid to spend time making new friends all day, eat good food and only having to actually work for a short time. If you get hired to be the main character, you might have to work a lot more, but you'd also be getting paid a lot more as well.

While living in Bangkok, I submitted my information including photos to several agencies, and then they would call me from time to time for different job opportunities. If you've got the time being an actor or model can be a great way to earn some side money.

Airline Employee

As you can imagine, if you work for an airline, there are

opportunities to live in foreign countries. Whether you are ground staff or a flight attendant, there are chances to move all over the world to consider.

Over my years of living abroad, I have met tons of flight attendants. If you become a flight attendant, don't expect to have a ton of time in each country that you visit. I've heard tons and tons of stories of long working hours without much free time, to take in destinations. Working as ground staff might be a better option if you plan to spend more time in one country.

Online Marketer

For about five years, I was an online marketer and had my own firm that managed several clients on a monthly basis. If you know about online marketing already, this might be a perfect career path to simply jump right into. If you don't, no need to fear, all of the resources are available online, just like becoming a web developer!

When I had my online marketing business, I focused on search engine optimization, also known as SEO. Search engine optimization is the process of making a website perform better in search engine results such as Google, Bing or Yahoo. Each search engine uses a different set of criteria in ranking its database of websites in the search results.

My services provided optimization so when a

prospective customer searches for a business, the business's website would appear high in the search results. The target for everyone is to be on the first page of the search results when related keywords are searched for. Obviously, this is a very valuable service as it will directly increase targeted traffic for the business. If you are able to prove that you can bring value, I'm sure that you will have unlimited clients knocking down your door.

Make sure you have proof illustrating the effectiveness of your hard work to show to your future clients. It's hard to ignore compelling data! Online marketing gives complete control of where you can work from, how many hours you work and how much you charge.

Over the years, I found that the business model that works best is when you have clients kept on a monthly payment basis. This will provide financial stability so you won't feel uneasy about where your next income is coming from.

My business was very successful financially, but what drew me away from online marketing, in the end, was constantly dealing with the clients. I enjoyed the freedom that it offered, but I didn't enjoy being told what to do by people that had paid me to handle their marketing efforts. If you hire a professional why wouldn't you just let the professionals do their job?

Social Media Manager

Another active income opportunity that is closely related to online marketing and web development is social media management. These days, people who have the basic skills to use social media could also quite easily learn how to professionally manage it, without too much additional effort. However, to become a successful social media manager, you really have to know how to grow a social media account through the best ways possible.

There are several skills required to be a successful social media manager. First, you have to understand the concepts of marketing and branding to make sure the company appears in a certain way online. Second, a social media manager has to understand how to grow a social media account through targeted engagement. Finally, once you are confident with your skills, you'll need to know how to network to get clients.

It's important to put together a portfolio of your work to show to prospective clients. The service is generally provided as a monthly service which will give you a stable income. My recommendation would be to focus on techniques that bring your clients the most value for their money.

There are many less legitimate techniques out there that don't bring anyone real value. I'm talking about artificially inflating followers and engagement which isn't ethical and not recommend. No matter what we do, we need to offer real value!

Guesthouse Staff

When I first moved abroad again, after graduating from university, I became a worker for a couple of months in exchange for accommodation at a guesthouse in Osaka, Japan. What they hired me for was to be the English-speaking staff member. This basically meant that I just had to be around and be able to speak English with Japanese guests in order for them to practice. Getting free accommodation for speaking my native language sounded pretty good to me.

In exchange for my amazing ability, I was given my own private room, and even some food was included. This was fantastic, and if you have the time, it's an opportunity that you may want to explore. If you can reduce or remove your accommodation cost, you will be way ahead of the game.

During this time, I had a fairly flexible "work" schedule. I could work on projects of my own while I was staying there and just had to take occasional breaks to speak English. If you are personable and wouldn't mind living in a guesthouse, then this is definitely something to consider. Start by writing a proposal and then sending it out to each of your potential targets. Make each email personal so that it doesn't look copy and pasted to increase your success rate.

Au Pair (Domestic Helper)

Much like how I've met many flight attendants abroad, I've also met many au pairs. If you're unfamiliar, this is a man or woman who is hired to take care of domestic duties at a house, mainly focused on child care, but could also include light housework. Generally, they are not paid much but given their accommodation and food in exchange for their assistance.

I have heard that this is generally a little more taxing than a guesthouse work exchange, but you'd be earning money as well, not just working on a barter exchange. Having cost of living eliminated will greatly alleviate your income requirements, but this work will not allow for as much free time.

I have heard many, both good and bad stories, from au pairs; it all really comes down to your host family, so if you go this route, choose a loving and caring family, not an evil one. At the end of the day, this could work out to a very good situation, but it is so important to do the research first.

Tour Guide

As I travel more and more, I attend more and more amazing tours in the process. I have found that a majority of tours I attend add great value to my life, providing incredibly memorable and educational experiences as I move from country to country. Seeing this value made me consider becoming a tour guide myself.

If you have any specific knowledge about a place and its culture and are personable, there is a good chance that you'd be able to host a great tour in your new home country. The startup costs are generally quite low and will simply come out of the profit if you list your tour on a website like Airbnb or something similar. Most of the time, websites will take a small cut of your profit, but they will offer your experience to a vast audience that you simply wouldn't be able to access without them.

I would focus on making sure that your tour offers a huge amount of value for customers. If you give a unique tour experience, your tour will be recommended again and again. Word of mouth marketing is the strongest form of marketing.

The types of experiences you can create are simply endless. You'll have a huge amount of free time, but income will be restricted to where your experience takes place. This should equate to a very enjoyable business, offering the joy of constantly meeting new people and sharing a special bonding experience with them.

I'd like to pursue this someday!

Instructor

If you have a special skill or hobby that you can teach, there is a potential for becoming an instructor. Some of the more common international instructors I've seen while abroad are dance, music, sports, and cooking instructors.

Some of the most memorable classes that I've taken abroad were cooking classes. One that stood out in my mind was a fine dining cooking class in Greece. I was paired up with the chef that had worked in several high-end restaurants around the world who taught me how to create some incredible Greek dishes and the cooking techniques to make them.

If being able to work from anywhere is what you're looking for, becoming an instructor is a great choice. There are very low startup costs and very low barriers to entry which make this a possibility for almost anyone. Plus, you can accept cash payments, cha-ching!

Translator

Are you fluent in more than one language? If you are, you might have an opportunity to become a language translator. I have met a handful of translators as I travel and live abroad. There are a lot of opportunities for work as a freelancer or working for a local company in your new country. I'd recommend trying it out as a freelancer first to see if it is something you'd actually enjoy doing.

Brainstorm your Own

If you're still struggling to come up with an active income idea after reading all of my recommendations, then I would recommend brainstorming ideas that fit you personally. I've used the following strategy time and time again to come up with business ideas that fit me, so I can do something I truly enjoy.

To start, make a list of your skills and don't limit yourself. Next, make another list of your hobbies and interests; make it as long as possible. Really go to town on these. Next, consider your ultimate goals and make a third list of job or business requirements such as freedom of work hours, low startup costs, freedom to travel, etc. Once you have your three lists listed, you can then begin to brainstorm potential business ideas.

Get creative and make a new list of business ideas that fit your skills, interests, and business requirements. Once you're done, you can rank them in order from most excitement to least excitement. At this point, you should have a decent list of options for businesses you could pursue.

Since you already know your total monthly living expenses from calculating it in previously, you can note down your income requirements. Consider how much you'd like to save each month too. For each viable business idea, calculate how much you could potentially earn monthly and see if it will meet your requirements for income. Be modest and underestimate potential income.

Finally, once you have greatly narrowed your business ideas down, you can break each business down into steps that would be required to take to get it up and running. Making a step-by-step guide for yourself will remove the guesswork and stress because tackling one step at a time is easier than looking at the entire obstacle without a real game plan.

Hopefully, this chapter on active income opportunities and the brainstorming strategies helped give you a few possible directions to take for your life of living abroad. Once you've made your final choices for businesses, I'd like to reiterate how important it is to make a game plan for yourself. A step by step plan will make it much easier to turn your dream into reality. Get as detailed as possible, so there is nothing left to chance.

In addition to your passive income, find something that you're excited to wake up every morning and work on to give your life purpose. There are an unlimited amount of active income opportunities available; the only restriction is your creativity. Choose something that truly excites you and don't simply play it safe. The majority of active incomes that I've listed offer complete freedom of time, location, and earning potential. Some of the opportunities have more built-in stability than others, but you can choose or come up with your own based on what feels best to your personality.

CHAPTER 8
LIVING STRATEGIES

In these last eight and a half years of living abroad, I didn't just sit around and waste my time away while in these exotic new lands. Since everything was always new, I was constantly forced to learn, which took me out of my comfort zone and made me a better person in the process. Along the way, through a marathon of extreme life-changing experiences, I was able to figure out the most efficient ways to get acclimated to new countries and how to live strategically to get the most out of the entire living abroad experience.

When I first began living abroad, I really didn't know anything about where I was moving or what I would do when I got there. Through trial and error, I found out what worked and what didn't because I had no other choice if I wanted to maintain my life abroad. For example, in the beginning, I didn't understand how to meet and network with people properly. It was very tough for me to expand my circle of acquaintances because I was too shy to talk to strangers. Over time, I have not only learned how to talk to people the correct way, but I've grown to become an extrovert. Now I've expanded my circle of friends immensely, not with fake friendships that fade away, but with meaningful lifelong relationships. This came directly from learning ways to connect with people quickly, which allows me to get past pleasantries, building a sense of comfort, so even if I've just met someone, I can get to a point where we feel like old friends in a relatively short time. These types of techniques have allowed me to make the most of my time living in foreign countries and thrive while doing so.

When people learn about my lifestyle of living abroad, after asking first how I manage my finances, the next most popular questions are all related to how I can overcome social challenges. These social challenges include how to learn a foreign language, how to devise a plan to get major goals accomplished, proper time management, and how to network. We will discuss strategies for these examples and many more in this chapter, so you too can thrive in your life of freedom and adventure abroad.

Journaling

I often overthink and get overwhelmed with all the ideas that I come up with. Sometimes, I'll have so much going on in my life that it will be hard to figure out which direction to go next. When I have a roadblock of confusion, I've learned that journaling is a great outlet to get my thoughts straight.

Putting my thoughts on paper has been a great technique to calm my mind, bring clarity, and make it easier to determine my future direction in life. There's something about physically taking a pen or pencil and writing on paper that is so therapeutic. I have tried typing my journals in the past, and it just doesn't have the same effect as handwriting.

No matter what is going on in your life, journaling will help bring clarity. There's never a bad time to journal. My technique for journaling starts with a period of brain-dumping. This is where I let everything that is on my mind out onto the paper; there is no filter. This is not the time to spell check or grammar check either; this is just time to let your thoughts out.

After the brain-dump is complete, I'll write a few things that I'm thankful for in life. As mentioned in the earlier chapters, being thankful is a major key to prolonged happiness and fulfillment. I'll jot down things that I am thankful for such as being alive, having a place to live, my health, family, or anything else that's on my mind. After everything has been let out onto the paper, I will feel a sense of calm and relief.

The next step would be to formulate a to-do list of things you'd like to overcome, big or small. Once you've made your list, brainstorm and figure out what you need to do next in life. This is easiest when challenges are broken down into smaller tasks, making the whole issue much easier to manage. Having a clear roadmap of how to get where you want to go will put the at mind ease.

If you have no destination in life, you'll never get to where you want to go. There needs to be a target to focus on, so we can work towards the bigger picture. If not, we are just spinning our wheels and stagnating.

Getting started is always the hardest part. However, journaling is actually a very easy practice, and once our thoughts are out on the paper, we have put ourselves in motion to get goals accomplished.

In the beginning, after first moving abroad, when we don't know anyone, everything is unknown; when we are completely depending on ourselves, stress may come along with an immense amount of excitement. These major life transitions, when stress arises, are the perfect time to focus on journaling to keep our minds happy. It's very important to manage stress and develop healthy habits, so we don't fall into any sort of negative thinking.

Whenever possible, it's important to clear our minds of

past and future worries; all we really have is this current moment in time that we have control over ourselves. No matter what happened in the past, or what will happen in the future, if it's not the present moment, then it's out of our control. Stressing about the past or future will not improve the present mental state. All we can do is work on techniques that bring peace and clarity such as journaling or an activity that brings us into the moment such as exercise or meditation.

Journaling helps clear up what is important and makes the things we have control over clear. Once a plan is laid out, we can overcome our obstacles with less stress. There are no rules when it comes to journaling, so don't be too hard on yourself when you're letting it out. Don't judge your thoughts. Let it out, and I promise you'll feel more at ease.

Daily Schedule

If you're new to working for yourself, it can be incredibly easy to get distracted when you're trying to get your things done. If you're working at home, it can be all too easy to lie down in bed and watch Netflix instead of working; I may or may not know from experience.

If you've set your goals through journaling, then if you're not getting those goals accomplished, what are you doing? If you go the entrepreneurial route, the thing to remember is that because you are now your own boss, you are the only limiting factor for what can be accomplished. There is nobody to blame for progress or setbacks but yourself. If you get distracted and procrastinate your work, only you will suffer. There's a sense of freedom that comes with knowing that you're your only limitation. You can be incredibly productive and overcome the largest goals you never thought possible if you go about it in the right way.

I've learned that following a daily schedule keeps me on track so that I can be the absolute most productive as possible. Yes, I still occasionally wander off and spend 45 minutes on YouTube, but when I snap out of it and remember my schedule, I get right back on task! What I learned is that it's important to set aside time when you're at most your most productive and focused time during the day. For me, this tends to be in the morning from 5 am to 12 noon.

Therefore, as soon as I wake up, I'll just bang out as much work as I can and focus on the tasks with the highest priority until noon. After lunch, I have more trouble staying focused and don't work as efficiently, so I will change to tasks that still need to be done but that are also less on the priority scale.

In the afternoon and evenings, I also focus on my personal health and personal development. I'll discuss the importance of fitness, especially while transitioning to this lifestyle a little later. However, when it comes to scheduling it, I try to plan working out before a meal, so I can immediately eat after.

To stay productive during your designated work period, it's important to eliminate all distractions. This means putting your phone in airplane mode and hiding it somewhere far away from you; I lock mine away in another room. It wasn't until recently that I started logging how many times I checked my phone per day; the results were incredibly scary, so now I've focused on reducing my screen time. You might even need to turn your laptop into airplane mode as well if you find yourself not focusing.

In an average day, I tend to focus on my work for approximately 5 to 8 hours. We all have different productive working periods, but at the end of the day, the most important part is just having your schedule clear and written down, so you can stick to it. When we have complete freedom, we need to give our lives structure so we can stay focused.

I know it can be tough at first, but if you build a schedule that fits your personality, you'll be able to focus and attain your goals efficiently. It's important to always keep at the top of your mind that you are your only limiting factor. Simply remembering this and sticking to your schedule will keep you focused and less likely to procrastinate.

Language Learning

As mentioned, without fail, one of the questions I receive the most is how can I live somewhere if I don't speak the language. Most people seem to have language anxiety. They wrongly assume that if they don't speak a language, then they won't be able to function at all. Life doesn't just stop if you don't speak a language.

Fortunately, or unfortunately, it is almost always possible to survive in most countries only being able to speak English. This means you can survive, but it doesn't necessarily mean you can thrive. If you don't speak a language, you will be quite limited and forced to use a lot of body language to get what you want. Day-to-day life may be possible, but on a larger scale, if you don't speak a language, you'll always be stuck on the outside. For example, when I first arrived in Thailand, things felt very magical, and this feeling lasted for a long time.

Ignorance is bliss.

I later realized that a lot of this came from not speaking Thai language. When you don't know what's going on around you, things might seem better than they are in reality. It wasn't until I learned Thai language that I truly understood the culture and how things operated. If you want to learn deeply about the place you are in, which will ultimately benefit you more greatly, you'll need to know the language, but it doesn't have to be perfect.

Even if you don't become fluent in the target language, you will still realize immense benefits. When local people see that you're trying, they will increase their respect for you and be much more willing to help in tough situations. Learning how languages are formulated will help you get into how the locals think.

Over the years, I've gone through the process of learning several languages. I haven't become fluent in all of them, but I know enough to get by and make people smile, which is a very important thing to me. There was a time when I focused on learning Thai language and did end up becoming fluent. This was in that private school in Bangkok that I mentioned earlier. As years go by and I don't use it as much, I do lose some of the vocabulary temporarily. However, every time I return to Thailand, the Thai vocabulary finds its way back into my head, which is comforting knowing that you don't lose it forever.

Lucky for you, over my many years of learning languages, I didn't only study the languages themselves, I also studied how I could learn a language as quickly as possible. There are several techniques which I have identified that will have you quickly communicating your target language. My techniques are focused on speed, efficiency, and effective communication while placing grammar at a lower priority.

Language Learning Strategy

After learning several languages, I learned that nearly every language has about 500 most commonly used words that account for about 80% of day-to-day situations. Therefore, to achieve a level of effective communication all one must do is memorize those 500 most commonly used words.

If you're wondering, yes, when you speak your grammar might sound a little funny if you only know vocabulary words. Regardless of grammar, you will be able to understand a majority of what's being said and also able to get your point across. As an example, if someone learning English came up to me and said, "I go store" I would understand their meaning even if they didn't say "I'm going to the store." Yes, it does sound a little bit funny not to have perfect grammar, but in the beginning, this will be a lifesaver and allow for effective communication. Proper grammar will be focused on after the most essential vocabulary is built.

Before we start learning the 500 most used words, we must take note of how we say them. If you understand the words that are spoken to you, that is great, but in order to speak them and have people understand you, it's important to speak with correct pronunciation. Therefore, the very first step I recommend is learning the correct pronunciation of the alphabet or characters in your target language.

For languages with smaller alphabets such as Latin-based languages, it should be rather quick to memorize the correct pronunciation of each letter. Even with languages like Chinese and Japanese that have extensive character sets, which I have studied, there are methods to learn accurate pronunciation quickly, so don't be scared. Whatever learning process you find, be sure to use one that has an audio component. Some language learning books do a decent job of explaining the sound of a character or letter but confirm it is correct with audio before you develop saying it the wrong way. There are also lots of software and apps out there that allow you to record yourself saying it so you can hear the differences between you and a native speaker.

Once you feel proficient with your pronunciation, then it's time to smash the 500 most used vocabulary words into your skull. For vocabulary learning, old-fashioned flashcards tend to be the best way to go. You can either create physical flashcards or use digital flashcards such as Quizlet or Anki, which are both available online for free.

In tandem to the flashcards, you can also use free language learning apps such as Mango Languages or Duolingo, which not only teach you vocabulary words but also basic grammar. I found that learning these in tandem work great and allow me to build up a large swath of vocabulary in a short time. This is because the programs are like games and quickly link concepts together in your brain to help retain all the information efficiently.

It should be easy to find premade sets of flashcards online with the most common vocabulary words. If you're studying regularly, you should be able to memorize 10 to 20 words per day. As you learn, be sure to review as you go to make sure you don't forget the ones you've already learned. If you continue at this rate 10 to 20 words per day, you should be able to memorize the most commonly used 500 words in 1 to 2 months. Literally, anyone can do it; all it requires is a little self-discipline.

For my strategy of memorizing words quickly, the most important advice is to link the word with something you know already. For this, I use mnemonics, which are any learning technique that aids information retention or retrieval. The more connections you can build between the new information and information you already know, the easier it will be to remember what you are learning. Get creative with this; it doesn't have to make sense to others as long as it makes sense to you. This is generally done through auditory forms by linking the sounds of the new word or letter you're attempting to memorize with words in your native language. The overall gist of this is to simply link every new concept with what you already know, and you will memorize it much easier.

Once you get your vocabulary bank memorized, I recommend watching television shows in your target language. No matter how advanced language learning software has become, there still tends to be a disconnect between what type of speech they will teach you and what is most commonly used in day-to-day life. If you don't understand any slang in your target language, then you will be severely crippled when it comes to everyday conversation. That's why watching television in your target language will help you to understand what people are saying even when it's not in the dictionary.

Once you've taken the time to learn correct pronunciation and the most commonly used vocabulary, the next step is to learn proper grammar. I found that when it comes to grammar, learning it with a great textbook is the easiest and most efficient way. You can continue to use your apps in tandem, but at the end of the day, a quality grammar book will teach you way more extensively.

Ideally, at this point, you can hire a professional teacher or find a free language exchange partner that will go through the book with you to explain any concepts you need help with. While living in Korea and Japan, I met regularly with language exchange partners that answered all of my difficult language questions that I couldn't find answers to elsewhere. Keep in mind that with a language exchange partner you will be responsible to also teach that person English in return.

If you have the budget for a teacher or class, you will be

able to cover far more ground much quicker as a professional has their system down and won't waste your time, hopefully. Even people with the most self-discipline can get distracted at times; that's why it's important to have a time set aside for learning. Having a language partner or lesson with a regular schedule is a requirement as far as I'm concerned.

It only took me 6 to 7 months to become fluent in Thai language while studying five days a week at 2 to 3 hours per day. While in China, I had a private teacher for 2 to 3 months and was impressed by the amount I was able to learn.

In the end, learning a language is very valuable and will help you gain a much deeper understanding of where you are living. The transformation that took place in quality of life from not understanding to becoming fluent was incredible and well worth every bit of study time.

Networking Strategy

No matter where you are in life everything becomes a lot easier the more people you know. I'm not saying you need to meet every single person, but most opportunities happen in life because of a personal connection with someone else. It's important to have a solid network everywhere, but even more important when you are new in a foreign country.

When you arrive, you won't have anyone to ask for anything. The quicker you can build up a network of people, the better off you will be. People asked me if I ever become lonely while I'm living abroad or traveling, and the answer is never. This is because of two major factors. One is because I am an introvert naturally, so I don't mind spending a lot of time alone focusing on all of my projects which give my life meaning. The second factor is that I have developed very effective networking strategies that help me to meet and to know people quickly no matter where I am in the world.

I've found that instead of becoming lonely, I often create the opposite problem for myself and schedule too many appointments. If you have a lot of project work to get done, but you're always spending time meeting people, then it will be really easy to become distracted; there has to be a balance between focusing on work and networking. It's no good if you finish the week and you realize that instead of working you were meeting people for coffee every day.

Techniques for Meeting

Nowadays, with modern technology, meeting people has become the easiest it's ever been. When I started, there were a lot fewer apps and websites available for meeting to network or date people. Some of these apps did exist, but there was a stigma surrounding several of them, and they had a much lower number of users. As time goes on, I've witnessed a large growth in using the internet to meet people. Instead of having a stigma, it's now incredibly common. I guess I was just ahead of the curve on this one.

These days you don't need any courage whatsoever to send out a message online to a stranger. Imagine what it was like before cell phones; I do because I focused on meeting people face-to-face, which requires a completely different process. Let's start by discussing the easy route of networking online. Apps I've used in the past include CouchSurfing, Tinder, Hello Talk, Bumble, Happened, MeetUp, Facebook, and Instagram. These days the list goes on and on.

There are many negative parts of social media that have been rearing their heads lately such as enforcing negative biases, but what social media has always done a decent job at is bringing people together, if we use it with that intent. I've met several girlfriends online as well as made good friends.

Even though in the past some of the apps I listed were initially meant for dating, some have widened their focus to include a friendship networking feature. Don't worry; people not interested in dating are welcome abroad as well. That being said, the friendship part is a little bit harder because people seem less receptive, but it can still be done.

The Golden Rule

There is one technique I use which is crucial when getting to know people deeply, listening. When you've talked for a while online and have finally decided to meet in person, do your best to focus on them and not blab on about yourself the entire time. Listen to them deeply, ask questions to keep them talking, and soak up their information like a sponge. It's impossible to learn anything when your mouth is open. When people are talking, they feel more comfortable, especially when people are showing interest in them. Showing an interest in someone is very easy to do and will help attract people to you and not repel them like talking too much does.

A behavior that drives me nuts is when the person you are talking to isn't focused on the conversation. If you put your phone on the table, it shows that the person in front of you is secondary in importance to your phone. Whenever your phone rings, or there's notification and you check it, this is proven. Keep your phone put away and keep it on silent to give the person who has sacrificed their time to meet you. Everyone's time is extremely precious and should be respected.

For the first twenty years of my life, I really didn't have any social skills. It was sad. It wasn't until my first study abroad program in Bangkok which gave me a strong shove out of my comfort zone. This push gave me real confidence to finally approach and talk with strangers.

I still remember the first time my friends pushed me to talk to a cute girl near my campus in Bangkok. It was at a mall called Chamchuri Square where lots of students spent time outside of class. Imagine a young, 20-year-old trembling Pierre with a Chulalongkorn University uniform on, palms wet from sweat like I just washed my hands. There was a lot of hesitation on my part, but my friends wouldn't accept no for an answer, so I pulled it together and went up to her. I remember the walk up, my heart beating so fast, butterflies filled my stomach. I reached her and mustered up some sort of very non-smooth greeting, and she replied that she didn't speak English. Pretty hilarious right? The point was that I was able to face my fears and overcome them.

As I moved around the globe, I had a goal to keep improving my social skills and boost my confidence level. I sought out uncomfortable situations to make myself better. While living in Hong Kong, I created a game for myself. Since I had a lot of free time, I would simply go out and walk around areas such as Central and start conversations with women. This built my confidence and gave me a good deal of exercise. I'll admit that you'd probably only be best to use this approach for dating because it might be a little weird to approach in this manner for friendship. Nothing is impossible I guess.

Regardless of your intentions, talking to strangers will help build up a lot of confidence, especially if you're a shy person. Going up to strangers and simply saying hello as you walk by is a great place to start. After you're comfortable with that, then you can stop someone and start talking to them. Remember, that if someone denies you, it doesn't reflect on you, just let it go and move onto the next, there is no contract that forces someone to talk to you.

Over time, I learned that rejection doesn't need to mean anything negative. The only thing we do have control over is how we react. We are in control of our happiness in all circumstances. We can choose peace, regardless of what people say to us.

Gaining confidence has spilled over into many other parts of my life, like giving me the courage to pursue my dreams. I'm not scared of what people think when I create something because I've made it over all these hurdles that made me stronger.

Push yourself into the unknown, work on yourself, make yourself stronger.

Stay Healthy

The whole process of moving to a foreign country tends to bring stress and anxiety with it. It's easy to get overwhelmed with our new lives, so it's important to take the necessary steps to keep ourselves healthy, both physically and mentally. You won't get much accomplished if you're depressed or put on a bunch of weight.

I've found that by prioritizing my physical and mental health, it has allowed me to more easily achieve the goals that I've set for myself. I find that when I do less physical activity, I tend to have a more negative outlook on life. Not only more negative thoughts, but I also tend to overthink things if I'm not exercising.

Exercising regularly and staying fit lead to a more positive mental state naturally. I've never regretted going to exercise; I've always felt much better after. To feel our best, we must not only have a good level of physical fitness but also need to get regular sleep. If we take care of our bodies, our minds will think in a more positive way and this will greatly improve our chances of achieving our dreams.

I've broken down some of the strategies that I use to keep my body healthy like a well-oiled machine so I can get the most out of life!

Diet

For a lot of my life, I felt sluggish and tired throughout the day, and couldn't figure out the cause. My energy levels would vary between extreme highs followed by

dramatic crashes that took a while to recover from.
When I had high energy, I was very productive, but then
when I would crash, I could barely get anything done.
I'd typically end up losing all motivation to work and
would take a nap.

It took me many years to finally figure out why this was
happening. It turned out that the more processed
carbohydrates I ate, the worse I felt. For example, if I ate
a big meal of noodles and meat, I would crash shortly
after I finished eating. Other carbohydrates that have the
same effect are bread and rice. I found when I ate less
processed foods like vegetables and meat I didn't have
these immense energy swings. The problem is that the
processed carbohydrates digest quickly, spiking glucose
levels which are followed by a huge crash as your body
is working hard to digest the food. When I finally
realized that these items were the culprit, I was
incredibly relieved.

Now when I eat, I focus more on raw ingredients which
don't produce crazy roller coasters of energy. Keeping
the energy level at a constant allows for much greater
productivity with whatever I'm focused on. This
basically means eating more vegetables, fruits, and less
sugar and processed carbohydrates.

Any food that is processed too much by humans
generally becomes unhealthy. Over time, eating these
processed foods wreak havoc on our bodies, increasing

the rates of disease and shortening our life spans.

By focusing on eating more fresh and natural ingredients, we feel better both physically and mentally. The masses don't seem to realize how bad processed food is. It's probably too convenient and cheap, but you are what you eat. So, if you feed yourself processed garbage too much, then that's what you will become.

Cooking may take a little longer, but you'll be able to create food that you know you like and is healthy too. We must take care of our own bodies because nobody else is going to do it for us. We only have one body, so we better take care of it. Overall, we need to reduce processed foods and increase natural foods, and we will feel healthier, happier, and able to overcome life's biggest challenges.

Intermittent Fasting

Developed countries are becoming fatter and fatter as the rates of eating poor quality processed food increases. We are constantly bombarded with food consumption in modern society. In nature, animals are not constantly eating. Studies have shown that if we reduce our eating, down to a shorter period during the day, our bodies will benefit immensely.

In nature, animals go long periods in between eating, like we did before food was everywhere we turned.

During those down times, our bodies could rest and had a chance to rebuild their cells so they could better fight off problems such as disease in the future.

Intermittent fasting is simply reducing the time that we intake calories. The longer you go, to an extent, without eating during the day, the better your body will perform. To clarify, this is not starving yourself; this is simply extending the period without eating in the morning and the evening. In your eating window, you can eat just as many calories as you would normally eat, assuming that it's the healthy amount, which would be less than 2,000 calories per day for a man and less than 1,500 calories per day for a woman.

This small tweak in when you eat has massive benefits including increasing lifespan and reducing your risk of cancer.

   A. Blood levels of insulin drop notably, which improves fat burning, and reduces the risk of type 2 diabetes (1).

   B. The body induces cell repair processes, like removing waste material from cells which better prepare them to manage problems (2).

   C. Reduction of overall levels of inflammation, which are known to cause all sorts of health problems (3, 4, 5).

D. Blood levels of growth hormone may increase as much as 5 times (6, 7). Higher levels of growth hormone facilitate fat burning, muscle gain, and other benefits (8, 9).

E. Beneficial changes in several genes related to longevity and protection against disease and reducing cancer risk (10, 11).

On average, I go 17 to 18 hours a day without consuming any food. This means eating from around 12 noon to 7 pm. It doesn't have to be this exact window, but the longer the window, the better the results. If you have self-discipline and don't want to alter your eating window, you can alter this to fasting for two days a week where you restrict calories down to 500 or 600 calories per day and experience many of the same benefits.

If you're trying to lose weight, this habit will help you reach your optimum weight too because reducing the number of meals in most cases will reduce your overall calories for the day. After taking this new habit on for a while, you'll feel less bogged down, have more energy, and you won't feel as hungry during the fasting period. The hard part is starting, but if increasing your quality of life and overall lifespan are the benefits, then I think it's very worthwhile to put up with slight discomfort to start this habit.

Exercise

On days where I get very bogged down with overthinking, I find that if I go for a walk or do some exercise, I tend to feel way better. I've never had a time where I did some exercise where I didn't feel better afterward. It just doesn't happen. If you like to exercise, then it should be easy for you to make time for it every day.

If you don't, it doesn't have to be anything strenuous; a simple walk will help put your mind in a positive state. Walking around for 30 minutes to an hour, breathing in the fresh air, exploring a new area will always bring positive energy. Apparently, sitting down too long during the daytime is linked with all types of ailments, so it's important to keep moving.

Get up often while you're working. When I'm making my coffee or tea, I like to do squats and other quick exercises to help loosen up and feel better. You don't have to become a bodybuilder but doing regular physical activity throughout the day will always put your brain in a positive state, so don't skip it.

Meditation

Another way I take care of my mind and body is through meditation. When I was a young teenager, I first learned about meditation. I came across a yoga video online which was about an hour long; the last 10 minutes were a guided meditation. At that time, I would alternate days of practicing yoga and going for a 30-minute run.

Meditation has become one of my strongest tools to calm myself down. Unfortunately, a lot of people are quick to write off meditation as something they just can't do. When I talk to people about it, I often hear, "I can't just sit still." That's complete hogwash if you ask me. Why would someone write something off before even giving it a go?

It only takes a few minutes of meditation to see some of the amazing benefits. If you are one of those people that think that they cannot meditate, I believe that you are the type that would benefit the most. The feeling that you can't sit still will be completely erased by meditation.

Left to our own devices, our minds will keep running around like crazy little monkeys. If we can't practice self-control to overcome the crazy monkey mind, then we won't be able to be as productive and positive as possible. We will be slaves to our own brains. Hear me out and give it a shot.

How to Meditate

The technique for learning how to meditate is actually very simple. First, get comfortable, take a seated position, usually sitting on a pillow, cross-legged works best. If this is uncomfortable, you probably need more stretching in your life, but for now, sit on a chair.

Now, correct your posture, sit up straight, pretend there is a string pulling up through the top of your head, maintain good posture but don't be overly stiff. Your hands can rest on your knees. Third, close your eyes and take in a slow deep breath. As you breathe, do your best to focus on the inhalation and the exhalation. I try to elongate how long it takes to inhale and exhale and I hold for a few seconds at the end of each. The objective during this focus on your breathing is to stay in the present moment and not allow your mind to drift off to start being a little monkey again.

Focus on your breathing and focus on the sounds in the room to keep yourself in the moment. Notice all the sounds around you, the air conditioner or heater, the car passing by, the birds chirping, etc.

As soon as thoughts begin to come into your brain, gently guide yourself back to the moment by focusing on your breath and sounds around you. The process of drifting off and having to bring yourself back to the moment will happen multiple times, and that is fine. It's impossible to completely overcome your mind wanting to think, the goal is to limit the excess thinking as much as possible.

Over time, this process will become easier and easier; all those excessive thoughts will become much easier to control, and a sense of euphoria will come over you. Just 5 to 10 minutes of this exercise can bring immense mental clarity. Meditation can be so simple. If you're able to do this just a few times a week, regularly, obstacles in life will be much easier to overcome with your relaxed and positive thinking. The solution to all your problems will become much clearer, and it will be easier to decide on which direction to take.

Cultural Exploration

Wherever you end up living abroad, the focus should always be to learn about the place you are in and its culture. All too often, I witness expats and travelers surrounding themselves with other foreigners, who are just like them. Instead of truly experiencing the country they are in, they are experiencing a bubble world of familiarity. A coward's way. If you're not stepping out of your comfort zone to learn, then there isn't a point to move abroad. Instead of staying comfortable with what you know, focus on meeting local people and experiencing local culture as much as possible. It might be uncomfortable to push yourself at first, but you will ultimately be rewarded with a bounty of personal development.

One method I use to learn about local cultures is by joining tours and organized experiences. A lot of the time it would be very difficult to access local experiences unless you seek them out. Personally, whenever I go somewhere new, because I'm obsessed with eating and learning about food, I focus on experiencing food and drink tours which tend to give me a great insight into cultures and their histories. Some of my most memorable tours have been in Ljubljana, Athens, Tokyo, Seoul, Hong Kong, Guangzhou, Ho Chi Minh, Shanghai, and Beijing. I hope to go on a Belgian beer tour in the near future!

You don't have to be a food-obsessed freak like me; you can focus on tours about anything that truly excites you. Often, local organizations will organize experiences that don't cost money. Regardless if you pay or not, the point is to get together with a group of people that can teach you about culture. It will be rewarding, I promise.

Tours can easily be found through TripAdvisor, Airbnb, Facebook, Meetup, or a simple search. Each city generally has dozens of tours and experiences available, so there is no excuse not to try one. Taking the time to learn about something new has always been a very rewarding part of my life.

Avoiding Scams

In many places, as a foreigner, you'll stand out like a sore thumb. In some situations, this is not a problem, while in others, you'll become a target for opportunistic scammers. Whenever I'm walking around, and I see a tourist holding a giant paper map, I feel like they might as well draw a target on their back. It's like holding a sign that says, "Hey, look! I don't know what I'm doing."

Generally, if a stranger approaches you when you didn't request help, you should be wary of their intentions. This happens so much at airports and bus stations that I just completely ignore people that talk to me, no matter how persistent they are. Japan is the only place where I found this not to be the case. On my recent trip to Tokyo, someone approached me, and I ignored them, turns out they were just a volunteer, trying to help, I felt guilty after, oops.

Bad Taxi

The most common scams are the aggressive taxi drivers trying to get you to go with them. They will charge you so much more than the local rate. Avoid going with any taxi drivers who approach you, instead, walk to the taxi stand where the locals go. You can even ask locals for advice; they'll generally be more trustworthy than a hungry taxi driver. The whole mindset should be focused on how to blend in with the locals. Otherwise, you will become a target.

Pickpocket

Another very common occurrence is being pickpocketed. This is very common in crowded public areas like train stations or city centers. Simply put your money in places that are harder to get to and be aware of your surroundings at all times. I put my wallet inside my coat, in an interior pocket so it would be nearly impossible to grab without me noticing.

For women, it may be more difficult, but try to keep your valuables tucked away as best as possible. Perhaps consider a wallet over a purse while traveling. In Southeast Asian countries it's very common for people on motorbikes to drive by and snatch purses, sometimes dragging them to the ground in the process. Be careful; it can happen very fast.

In conclusion, it's important to live life in a meaningful way. Practicing the techniques I've outlined in this chapter, will guarantee that we are able to accomplish all of the goals that we set out to. Creating a plan for ourselves with journaling so we can constantly keep our goal in mind will make it much easier to achieve. After we have made our plan, it's important to give our lives structure by creating a daily schedule, so we don't procrastinate.

Becoming depressed will be a quick route to not achieving your goals, so it is incredibly important to take care of our physical and mental well-being. Journaling, meditation, and physical exercise will keep our bodies and minds in tip-top shape to propel us in the right direction. Being healthy both physically and mentally is like setting the foundation for building the Burj Khalifa. Your future rests on this foundation and will dictate all your future outcomes. Take care of yourself or risk achieving your dreams.

Taking time to seek out local experiences and meet good people along the way will add to your experience and lead to immense personal growth. You may find lifelong relationships in the process. Don't ever stay in your personal bubble; you will only miss out on opportunity after opportunity.

Push yourself out of your comfort zone constantly for the most benefit. If this shy little boy can transform into an extrovert, so can anyone else.

CHAPTER 9
EMBRACE THE UNKNOWN

From all my years of living and traveling around the world, I've gathered that most people would like to do the same. A life full of adventure and excitement is very attractive indeed. However, for a lot of people, it is a difficult task because they are stuck in their monotonous lifestyles and fear has frozen them in their tracks.

Many of us, when we look at the process of moving ourselves abroad and supporting ourselves completely, the whole lifestyle change can seem out of reach. My hope is that everyone can realize that if we break the whole process down, into manageable steps, it is completely possible to live abroad or accomplish any other big dream you have.

All of the strategies in *How to Live Abroad and Thrive with Passive Income* were meant to make the whole process more efficient. When I say anyone can do this, I really mean it. Like when people tell me that they can't cook, I respond with saying that anyone can follow a recipe. It's not that someone can't cook, it's that they won't try. The same thing goes with living abroad; the entire plan has now been laid out in front of you, very efficiently if I may say so myself, all you have to do is follow it. It's not hard, but it takes a small amount of courage to begin.

Until we step out of our comfort zones by giving ourselves the first shove, it will be hard to realize the benefits. Once we take the first step and start overcoming significant challenges, we will grow remarkably and become better people. The improvements will be very evident and overflow into all parts of our lives.

When we better ourselves by overcoming obstacles, we become wiser, stronger, and better equipped to take on whatever life throws at us. As you know, before I started living in foreign countries, I was young and shy and would hide away from my fears. After pushing myself hard when I was 20, I overcame all my greatest fears and challenges in my life and now embrace the unknown.

Without fail, every single time I've stepped out of my comfort zone, I've been able to improve myself in one way or another. Constantly seeking out new experiences makes life more exciting and rewarding and should be the ultimate encouragement you need to take the plunge and move abroad, especially now that you know how to do it. You're welcome; also thank you for your purchase.

The whole process comes down to the way we look at life. It's a common belief among most people that things are either good or bad. If we choose to change our thinking slightly, we can make all experiences into rewarding life lessons, regardless of how others may choose to classify them. Instead of saying things are good or bad, we can instead say that either thing good or a learning experience.

There really is no losing in life, only opportunities to grow and learn. Pursuing dreams of living abroad has the potential of breaking us down mentally. However, the big picture that must be kept in mind is that every single hardship we face will only make us stronger in the end. Every hardship will become a lesson and ultimately incredibly valuable.

Therefore, if we keep a positive attitude, it's impossible to "lose" by pushing ourselves out of your comfort zones and into the unknown. As long as we persevere, we will become better and more well-rounded individuals. Go for it.

More harm is done by indecision than wrong decision.

There's nothing more valuable in life than time. Time is

something that once it goes away, we will never get it back. In layman's terms, if you are in a position in life that you're not truly enjoying, perhaps it lacks excitement, such as an unfulfilling job, if you don't take steps to change your life's path, then time will simply pass you by, and the opportunity will be missed.

Don't allow yourself to be paralyzed by fear, the longer you wait, the more time that you will have wasted. For this reason alone, there is never a good reason to put off something we are truly passionate about, such as the dream of a life of adventure abroad.

At the end of the day, money is just an idea that humans came up with, in reality, it's mostly just paper. Don't allow pieces of paper to dictate life's most important decisions. There will always be opportunities to make more money, but there will never be an opportunity to make more time. Building a lifestyle of complete freedom of time is the ultimate wealth.

The only constant in life is that everything is guaranteed to change.

If you put off your move abroad to an undetermined future date, many changes in life could make it no longer possible. Your health may decline, your family may need your help, or some other external circumstance may make it impossible to pursue your dream of living abroad.

Don't put it off, take on this incredibly rewarding experience and have comfort in knowing that it will benefit you forever by challenging yourself and overcoming massive obstacles. If you don't, you'll instead be stuck with a lifelong regret of not pursuing your dream because you put it off for too long, until it became impossible. The only way to have no regrets is by pursuing your dreams immediately.

As soon as we make excuses, and put things off, we will surely have regrets later, and regrets are what we are working to avoid at all costs. The goal is to build lasting memories and personally develop, not create lasting regrets. You don't want to lie on your deathbed, thinking about all of the things you wish you would've done with your life. Wouldn't it be better to instead be able to look back over a lifetime of accomplishment in complete contentment?

You have the power to make your life meaningful, no one else. We must act now.

The whole process of deciding where to go, moving abroad, generating income and strategies of how to make the most of life abroad are all laid out for you in easily manageable steps. It's a piece of cake!

Knowing that there is nothing different between you or anyone else who has accomplished their biggest dreams is very important to keep in mind. In life, we are only in competition with ourselves. There's no reason to compare ourselves with others because we are all in different races. We must focus on being thankful for what we have and overcoming obstacles that stop us from getting where we want to go.

Key Points to Remember

When it comes to making the move abroad, one of the most important decisions of the whole process is making sure to choose a destination that is as unique as possible. Choosing a unique destination will set the foundation of the entire experience and will greatly increase your chances of personal development, which we are after.

When it comes to choosing your accommodation, the key point I'd like to reiterate is that you should find a good balance between living in both a convenient and affordable place. Accommodation costs, as we now know, are the most expensive costs of living anywhere. If we can find ways to minimize our rent or make it free, we can greatly reduce the amount of stress that comes from making money.

Generally, I've found that living farther away from a city center may be cheaper, but when you factor in costs of transportation and time, it may not be worth it. Be sure to challenge yourself by living around people that are local, not other foreigners.

Being frugal will alleviate stress now and in the future. Being able to save money is nearly as important as how much you are earning. No matter how much money you make, if you're not able to save, you'll never be able to get ahead. Make a budget you can focus on so you know how much you need to save and how much you need to earn.

While saving and investing, don't get greedy and try to grow your money too quickly. Generally higher risk equates to great reward potential, but those risks are usually not worth it, especially when factoring stress. You're better off, in the long run, to grow your money slow and steady and not lose your savings in the process.

Coming from me, a person who has lost a large amount of their savings in the stock market, I assure you, it's really not worth. Both your stress-free mind and your fat bank account will thank you later.

Adopting a minimalist lifestyle will help prioritize what is important in life and allow us to get the most out of life. When we focus less on consuming, we have more time to focus on attaining fulfillment from what truly matters. Material possessions keep us distracted and will lead us farther and farther away from our goals.

Once we make enough money to live comfortably, making and saving more will not make us any happier. I'm not saying we need to set our goals so low, that we are just scraping by, but it's important to find a balance.

Always wanting more is a mental sickness.

Always desiring things that you don't have is a problem that can be solved by appreciation. Being thankful and appreciative for everything will lead you to a life of abundance and fulfillment.

Although money shouldn't be the motive, we need it to survive in the current system. Building multiple streams of passive and active income is like building an insurance policy for yourself. When one fails, you'll have the other to cover you. This will reduce stress in your life because no matter what, you'll have some money coming in to cover your expenses. The investment of time to create a passive income stream will be completely worth it in the long run as it will pay off time and time again.

Strategizing properly by journaling is essential to attaining your goals. It's very important to lay everything out on paper to see it clearly. Only then can you create an all-encompassing plan to get where you want to go. The foundation for achieving your goals comes from being healthy. Not only is it important to have a healthy mindset, but also a healthy body.

Taking the time to learn about those around you is a guaranteed way to personally develop. That's why it's important not to surround yourself with other foreigners that think the same as you. Step out of your comfort zone, and you will be rewarded.

Life is all about persistence and not giving up. Remember there is only winning or learning; nothing is bad. Being able to get back up after you fall will eventually pay off by making you a better person. You can always find a creative solution to any issue. The clock is always ticking, all we have control over is the moment so don't put off what you want any longer, go after your dream now!

References

1. Leonie K Heilbronn, Steven R Smith, Corby K Martin, Stephen D Anton, Eric Ravussin; Alternate-day fasting in nonobese subjects: effects on body weight, body composition, and energy metabolism, The American Journal of Clinical Nutrition, Volume 81, Issue 1, 1 January 2005, Pages 69–73, https://doi.org/10.1093/ajcn/81.1.69

2. Alirezaei M, Kemball CC, Flynn CT, Wood MR, Whitton JL, Kiosses WB. Short-term fasting induces profound neuronal autophagy. Autophagy. 2010;6(6):702-10.

3. James B. Johnson, Warren Summer, Roy G. Cutler, Bronwen Martin, Dong-Hoon Hyun, Vishwa D. Dixit, Michelle Pearson, Matthew Nassar, Richard Tellejohan, Stuart Maudsley, Olga Carlson, Sujit John, Donald R. Laub, Mark P. Mattson, Alternate day calorie restriction improves clinical findings and reduces markers of oxidative stress and inflammation in overweight adults with moderate asthma, Free Radical Biology and Medicine, Volume 42, Issue 5, 2007, Pages 665-674, ISSN 0891-5849, https://doi.org/10.1016/j.freeradbiomed.2006.12.005

4. Aksungar F, B, Topkaya A, E, Akyildiz M: Interleukin-6, C-Reactive Protein and

Biochemical Parameters during Prolonged Intermittent Fasting. Ann Nutr Metab 2007;51:88-95. doi: 10.1159/000100954

5. "Mo'ez Al-Islam" E. Faris, Safia Kacimi, Ref'at A. Al-Kurd, Mohammad A. Fararjeh, Yasser K. Bustanji, Mohammad K. Mohammad, Mohammad L. Salem, Intermittent fasting during Ramadan attenuates proinflammatory cytokines and immune cells in healthy subjects, Nutrition Research, Volume 32, Issue 12, 2012, Pages 947-955, ISSN 0271-5317, http://www.sciencedirect.com/science/article/pii/ S0271531712001820

6. Ho KY, Veldhuis JD, Johnson ML, et al. Fasting enhances growth hormone secretion and amplifies the complex rhythms of growth hormone secretion in man. J Clin Invest. 1988;81(4):968-75.

7. M L Hartman, J D Veldhuis, M L Johnson, M M Lee, K G Alberti, E Samojlik, M O Thorner; Augmented growth hormone (GH) secretory burst frequency and amplitude mediate enhanced GH secretion during a two-day fast in normal men, The Journal of Clinical Endocrinology & Metabolism, Volume 74, Issue 4, 1 April 1992, Pages 757–765, https://doi.org/10.1210/jcem.74.4.1548337

8. Blackman MR, Sorkin JD, Münzer T, et al. Growth Hormone and Sex Steroid

Administration in Healthy Aged Women and Men: A Randomized Controlled Trial. JAMA. 2002;288(18):2282–2292. doi:10.1001/jama.288.18.2282

9. Rudman, Daniel, Feller, Axel G., Nagraj, Hoskote S., Gergans, Gregory A., Lalitha, Pardee Y., Goldberg, Allen F., Schlenker, Robert A., Cohn, Lester, Rudman, Inge W., Mattson, Dale E. Effects of Human Growth Hormone in Men over 60 Years Old 1990 New England Journal of Medicine 1-6 323 1. 10.1056/NEJM199007053230101 https://www.nejm.org/doi/full/10.1056/NEJM19 9007053230101

10. Mathew R, Karp CM, Beaudoin B, et al. Autophagy suppresses tumorigenesis through elimination of p62. Cell. 2009;137(6):1062-75.

11. Wolfe DM, Lee JH, Kumar A, Lee S, Orenstein SJ, Nixon RA. Autophagy failure in Alzheimer's disease and the role of defective lysosomal acidification. Eur J Neurosci. 2013;37(12):1949-61

Dear lovely readers,

Please support me by leaving a positive review wherever you have purchased this book!

Thank you!

Warmest regards,

Pierre Blake
PIERREBLAKE.com
@PIERREBLAKE

CPSIA information can be obtained
at www.ICGtesting.com
Printed in the USA
BVHW041350100820
586003BV00011BA/334

9 781093 246025